D1063876

HABERMAS'S CRITICAL THEORY OF SOCIETY

SUNY Series in the Philosophy of the Social Sciences
Lenore Langsdorf, editor

HABERMAS'S CRITICAL THEORY OF SOCIETY

Jane Braaten

State University of New York Press

Published by
State University of New York Press, Albany

Printed in the United States of America

For information, address State University of New York
Press, State University Plaza, Albany, N.Y. 12246

Production by Marilyn Semerad
Marketing by Bernadette LaManna

Library of Congress Cataloging-in-Publication Data

Braaten, Jane, 1956–
Habermas's critical theory of society : Jane Braaten.
p. cm. — (SUNY series in the philosophy of the social sciences)
Includes bibliographical references and index.
ISBN 0–7914-0759–4 (hardcover) . — ISBN 0–7914-0760–8 (papr.)
1. Habermas, Jürgen. 2. Critical theory. I. Title. II. Series.
HM22.G3H333 1991
301'.01—dc20

90–47708
CIP

10 9 8 7 6 5 4 3 2 1

The theory of communicative action is not a metatheory but the beginning of a social theory concerned to validate its own critical standards.

Habermas (*TCA* I, xxxix, 1984)

Developed forms of capitalism can just as little afford to live without the welfare state as to live with its further expansion.

Habermas, 1986

Contents

List of Abbreviations

CES — *Communication and the Evolution of Society,* trans. Thomas McCarthy (Boston: Beacon Press, 1979).

LC — *Legitimation Crisis,* trans. Thomas McCarthy (Boston: Beacon Press, 1975; original German edition published by Suhrkamp Verlag, 1973).

MCCA — *Moral Consciousness and Communicative Action,* trans. Christian Lenhardt and Shierry Weber Nicholson (Cambridge, Mass.: The MIT Press, 1990).

PDM — *The Philosophical Discourse of Modernity: Twelve Lectures,* trans. Frederick Lawrence (Cambridge, Mass.: The MIT Press, 1987; original German edition published by Suhrkamp Verlag, 1985).

TCA I — *The Theory of Communicative Action*, vol. I, *Reason and the Rationalization of Society,* trans. Thomas McCarthy (Boston: Beacon Press, 1984; original German edition published by Suhrkamp Verlag, 1981).

TCA II — *The Theory of Communicative Action,* vol. II, *Lifeworld and System: A Critique of Functionalist Reason,* trans. Thomas McCarthy (Boston: Beacon Press, 1987; original German edition published by Suhrkamp Verlag, 1981; 3rd corrected edition, 1985).

V *Vorstudien und Ergänzungen zur Theorie des kommunikativen Handelns* (Frankfurt am Main: Suhrkamp Verlag, 1984). "Preliminary and Supplementary Studies to the Theory of Communicative Action."

Introduction

Jürgen Habermas is now one of the most important living intellectuals on the European continent. Already acclaimed by a prominent German cultural commentator in 1969 as a leading scholar of astonishing range at the age of forty, in 1979 he was deemed by the West German news journal *Der Spiegel* to be "the most powerful thinker" in the nation. He has deeply influenced many of the current leading European figures both in philosophy and the *Sozialwissenschaften* (the social sciences and political theory) and has provoked discussion among psychoanalysts and educators. The efforts of Martin Jay, David Held, Richard Bernstein, Thomas McCarthy, and John Thompson in the 1970s and early 1980s to introduce Habermas to the English-speaking world have met with success, and his reputation in this country has been steadily expanding over the past two decades.[1] In addition, translations of a number of other contemporary German theorists, including some whose hypotheses have been adopted by Habermas, have been published over the past decade, owing to the efforts of McCarthy and others.[2] These translations extend our view of the German intellectual scene, revealing the high caliber of modern German debates on the legitimacy of the postindustrial capitalist welfare state. Finally, during the latter half of the 1980s, a number of extensive introductions and critical analyses of his more recent work have appeared on this side of the Atlantic.[3] These books are written in response principally to Habermas' latest attempt, in *The Theory of Communicative Action,* to chart the course for a theory of society that is at once explanatory and normative; a theory that stands "between philosophy and science";

and to his defense of this theory against the challenges raised by postmodernism in *The Philosophical Discourse of Modernity.* [4]

This book has the relatively modest aim of providing a brief, accessible introduction to Habermas's critical theory as it has taken shape since 1968. The core of his critical theory comprises two mutually complementary theories—the theory of communicative rationality and the theory of societal rationalization, whose joint development is the task of *The Theory of Communicative Action* (1981). This book is designed to reflect the core content of Habermas's theory and approaches his other work, both early and late, in relation to it. I focus almost exclusively on Habermas's theory, placing it in a historical context only in very general terms. Of course, it would be unwarranted to convey the impression that Habermas's theory, or indeed any systematic theory of societal evolution in the German tradition, has ever been an isolated undertaking. Ever since Hegel attempted to radicalize Kant's critique of reason by introducing historical and social dimensions, theories in this tradition, about how societal institutions evolve, have been conceived in response to other theorists. Knowledge of the history of the dilemmas and controversies to which Habermas responds further illuminates the profundity of his own theory. Therefore, I will encourage the interested reader to pursue the history of critical theory in several excellent sources elsewhere.[5]

Habermas inherits the efforts of German theorists, spanning the 200 years since Immanuel Kant, to come to terms with the arrival of modern society. The reasons for which "modernity" poses a problem at all are contested, but observers on both the Left and the Right have agreed that the emergence of capitalist parliamentary democracies has coincided with a loss of tradition and the moral and social stability that can be secured only by tradition.[6] For the Germans, the attempt to overcome this loss has entailed a continuing attempt to understand the relationship between *reason,* which the modern era has taken as the source of guidance for both its moral and scientific pursuits, and *autonomy,* which has become in the modern era the principal moral criterion for determining the legitimacy of social and political arrangements. For Kant, to act autonomously is to act rationally, and to decide rationally is to decide freely. However, to many, especially in this century, it has seemed as though autonomy is threatened by the process of 'rationalization' characteristic of modern societies. (This concern was first developed by the turn of the century German sociologist Max Weber.[7]) Closely linked to this concern is the question of well-being or happiness. It would seem that genuine freedom is bonded to the possibility of human happiness just as much as it is to the exercise of rationality. How, then, are these three ideals—reason, autonomy, and well-being—related? The intuition that the pursuit of each of the three depends on the pursuit of the other two is present in Marx's theory of history, as well as in that of Jürgen Habermas.

German philosophy and social science has long been most interested in locating the *telos* or aim of human society. Since Hegel's powerful argument that we are shaped by society, as well as shapers of society, it has been thought by Hegelians that reason itself is something that evolves, and that as it evolves, the ground rules of society change as well. The *telos* of human society is to be discovered by sifting through the patterns in these changes—patterns in our choices that reveal the character and direction of development, of human reason.

It is essential to a theory of societal evolution in the Hegelian legacy, such as Habermas's, that one can speak of a society as something that *learns.* This may be an unfamiliar premise to the American student, social theorist, or social scientist. Habermas's theory of societal evolution appears long after the global and systematic approaches inherited from Weberian 'classical' sociology (such as Talcott Parsons's structural functionalism) have been abandoned by mainstream American sociology, which now appears to have committed itself largely to the study of local social groups and phenomena.

Sociology in Germany, however, remains strongly connected to its origin as the 'theory of bourgeois society.' The theory of bourgeois society began as a response to an observed loss of tradition and community and increase in functional organization of society that occurred with modernization. Habermas writes: "To it fell the task of explaining the course of the capitalist modernization of traditional societies and its anomic side effects. . . . Almost without exception, the classical figures of sociological thought attempted to lay out their action theory in such a way that its basic categories would capture the most important aspects of the transition from 'community' to 'society'" (*TCA* I, 5) This transition from community to society is widely thought among German sociologists to have involved a fundamental shift in the kinds of norms that governed action from traditional norms to rationally defensible norms. For this reason, the 'basic categories' of sociology have been chosen with the aim of explaining a process of societal ***rationalization.***

Societal rationalization is a learning process. The hypothesis of a theory of societal rationalization is that, much as children cannot be taught to solve for equations unless they first have learned what a number is, societies cannot adopt certain kinds of institutions—which essentially, are systems of regulatory principles—without first agreeing that certain kinds of regulatory principles or norms are possible. For example, the norms of a secular and rationally based ethic will not prevail among a people whose actions are guided by tradition. This is not merely a matter of the necessity of learning new concepts; it has to do with the structure of traditional as opposed to post-Enlightenment, rationalized thinking. Traditional thought, according to this hypothesis, in certain fundamental ways is undifferentiated in comparison to modern thought, which attempts to found beliefs and convictions upon a rational basis.[8] Theories of societal rationalization propose some means by which evolving patterns in the expression of human rationality bring about societal change, in order to explain the observed tendency of premodern European societies to become modern societies. In short, theories of societal rationalization postulate that rationality is the most basic principle of historical change.

Habermas's theory of societal rationalization must be assessed from two distinct philosophical perspectives, for it contains both a theory or critique of rationality, in the Kantian tradition, and a theory of societal evolution in the Hegelian, Marxian, and Weberian traditions. Though these two aspects of Habermas's work are heterogeneous and require distinct modes of assessment, they are complementary, producing a theory that is at once critical and explanatory. A theory of rationality is a normative theory, and retains a critical potential when it is used in the explanation of actual history. But a theory of rationality also possesses explanatory potential, when employed in reconstructing the history of the 'choices' made by the societies in our past. It should now be evident that the structure of Habermas's theory is neither a familiar one, nor a simple one. For this reason, the following chapter will be devoted to sorting out the general relationship between these two 'aspects' of Habermas's theory, and what it is supposed to accomplish. For now, it should suffice to begin with this very general image of the theory.

Habermas's 'critical explanation' of the rise of modern capitalist society hypothesizes that it is the outcome of a process of 'one-sided rationalization.' This kind of argument, of course, can be made only if one has a picture of what rationalization would look like if it were not one-sided. For this purpose, Habermas employs an inclusive conception of rationality—what he calls *communicative rationality*. The critical content of his theory derives its normative force from this conception of rationality. At the same time, the theory of rationality also serves to explain the evolution of societal institutions, because it displays the fundamental constraints upon human choices, such as our choices of societal institutions.

Habermas has not always pursued just this hypothesis. Through the publication in 1968 of *Knowledge and Human Interests* and into the 1970s, Habermas's vision of modern society was less systematic, but held a clear affiliation to the critique of technocratic consciousness by his predecessors and mentors at the Frankfurt School for Social Research, or Frankfurt School—Max Horkheimer, Theodor Adorno, and Herbert Marcuse. Gradually he shifted away from the therapeutic analysis of the rise of the modern alienated consciousness, a project that belongs to what he refers to as the *philosophy of consciousness*. As the focus shifted from consciousness and false consciousness, his work became less a critique of ideology than a critique of the evolving economic, social, and cultural conditions of human interaction. The philosophy of consciousness is inadequate as a framework for the analysis of reason in Habermas's view, because reason is inherently based upon mutual commitments to standards of interaction or communication. In short, consciousness does not precede sociality. Instead, for Habermas, the exercise of our ability to communicate is constitutive of consciousness.

Habermas's conception of what makes his theory a critical theory now diverges significantly from the one, based upon Habermas's earlier work, so lucidly explained in Raymond Geuss's *The Idea of a Critical Theory.*[9] Geuss elucidates Habermas as a critic of ideology, a critic of false consciousness, who uses the possibility of perfectly undistorted communication as a vantage point for the critique of distorted communication. In the *Theory of Communicative Action,* however, Habermas decided not to pursue the development of critical theory in this form, hinting that it is not possible for ideologies to establish a hold over modern societies.[10] Instead, he thinks, the prevalence of asociality and the lack of genuine autonomy in modern society is due to certain patterns in the ways that modern institutions shape and are shaped by communication or social interaction.

The first half of this book is devoted to explaining Habermas's theory of rationality, which is the core of his social theory and method. Before examining the basic standards of rationality in Chapters 2 and 3, the following chapter first gives an overview of Habermas's critical theory and its stance relative to other theories in the tradition of Kant and Hegel. Because it is so important to Habermas's theory of society that his theory of communicative rationality be well established, three full chapters are devoted to it. The chapter divisions reflect the division of the theory of communicative rationality into three types of justification: the defense of truth claims in theoretical (scientific and philosophical) discourse, normative validity claims, and aesthetic validity claims. In keeping with Habermas's social theoretical use of the consensus theories of truth, normative validity, and aesthetic validity, he develops these accounts as accounts of what the meanings of the terms 'truth', 'normative validity', and 'aesthetic validity' are, *given the role that these notions play in actual communication and social interaction.* One might say, then, that a major condition that a theory of truth, normative validity, or aesthetic validity must fulfill, according to Habermas, is that it be capable of accounting for our actual verbal action.

Chapters 2 through 4 attempt to assemble and clarify the arguments that Habermas gives in defense of the consensus theories of truth, normative validity, aesthetic validity, and the theory of communicative rationality as a whole, and to present them in a way that speaks to some of the important concerns of the American student of philosophy or social science. The questions that are addressed in these chapters are more familiar to the philosophically trained reader than to others. I have attempted to present the issues in a way that is accessible to a broader audience, without sacrificing depth, with the hope of illustrating to readers whose background is in, say, social or political science the importance that the concept of rationality holds in the European *Sozialwissenschaften.*

In addition to introducing the aesthetic validity claim, Chapter 4 gives a critical review of Habermas's arguments that there are universal rules of language usage (a universal pragmatics), and that these provide the groundwork for a conception of communicative rationality. This chapter is the pivot of the book. The theories of truth, normative validity, and aesthetic validity are constitutive of the the theory of communicative rationality. Moreover, as I shall argue, the argument in support of normative force of Habermas's discourse ethics is given in his defense of the latter theory.

The conception of communicative rationality defended here provides the foundation of his philosophy of social science and the theory of societal rationalization that is envisioned in it. Just as the consensus theories of the validity claims are to explain certain aspects of speech action, the theory of communicative rationality as a whole is to be used to explain how social interaction in general is possible and, a fortiori, the evolution of specific social arrangements and institutions. Of course, this explanatory power obtains only if the account of communicative rationality is an adequate account of rationality. The first three chapters introduce Habermas's defense of his accounts of the specific validity claims, but it must also be shown that a commitment to consensus underlies every communicative act. The argument for this general claim is reconstructed in this chapter.

The second part of this book pertains to his philosophy of social theory, which proposes a preliminary outline of and a method for a theory of societal rationalization. Chapter 5 begins with a description of the method that he proposes for the construction of a theory of the rationalization of modern society. The method is intimately connected to his distinction between strategic, functional, and communicative rationality. It is a dual method, designed to analyze and explain societal evolution from two perspectives, distinguished by the concept of rationality that each employs. Once these two perspectives have been explained, it will be possible to explain Habermas's diagnosis of modern society. Finally, I assemble his reasons for rejecting other possible approaches to the construction of a theory of societal rationalization.

Chapter 6 surveys Habermas's responses to two challenges: positivism (which still figures strongly in the heritage of current American philosophical debates), and the postmodernist critics of Habermas's 'modernism.' The second part of this chapter gives an overview of Habermas's exhaustive defense of the 'modernist' commitment to reason against its 'postmodern' critics in his *The Philosophical Discourse of Modernity.* This aspect of Habermas's work is of great significance, because it brings to the fore the fact that Habermas is not merely proposing a new sociological method or philosophical theory, but is a contender, with the postmodernists, in shaping our evolving understanding of modernity and its future.

Finally, Chapter 7 engages in an assessment of Habermas's critical theory, by looking at three critical applications of his theory in the United States. One of the conclusions to be drawn from them is that, although Habermas has not lent much importance to the critique of ideology or to remaining class conflicts in his theory, there are ways that even his recent theory can be applied in critical analyses of remaining ideological and class issues.

It is hoped that the overall plan of this book will further elucidate that feature of Habermas's work which puzzles so many of those whose philosophical or social scientific training goes lightly on Germanic approaches; namely, the location of critical theory 'between philosophy and science.' On the one hand intended to provide a critique of rationality, Habermas's work, on the other hand, also applies that analysis of rationality in an explanation of the evolution of modern societal institutions. This approach to social science is unusual in Britain and the United States and is often viewed as speculative. Although this book is intended more as an introduction to than as a defense of Habermas's critical theory, I hope, by presenting it as a credible theory, to engage the interest of the reader in the role of the concept of rationality in explanations of societal change.

CHAPTER 1

An Outline of Habermas's Critical Theory

Jürgen Habermas's critical theory of society is a diagnostic theory of societal rationalization. A theory of societal rationalization is a theory that explains the evolution of modern society out of premodern traditional societies as a process of rationalization. Societal rationalization is generally understood either as a process in which institutions increasingly tend to secure the acceptance of society by appeal to rationally justifiable principles rather than to tradition, or as a process in which society becomes increasingly capable of appropriating nature to meet its expanding needs and interests. The former characterization is often associated with Max Weber, the prominent nineteenth century German sociologist who explained the rise of capitalism as a product of the Protestant ethic. The latter characterization is associated with Karl Marx. Both Weber and Marx, along with the Frankfurt School theorists Theodor Adorno and Max Horkheimer, and Habermas himself owe much to the precedent established by Georg Wilhelm Friedrich Hegel's attempt at reconstructing the history and structure of consciousness in modern society.

As a *critical* theory, Habermas's theory of societal rationalization is intended not only to explain the process by which modern capitalist society evolved, but also to reveal the nature and causes of its systematic failures. Unlike (ideal) psychoanalytic theories and Habermas's own earlier work (up through *Knowledge and Human Interests*), his recent work is not aimed at finding a way out of the problems confronting modern society by providing either an explanation or a critique of ideology. Its explanation of societal evolution, then, could be characterized as a *diagnostic* explanation, as opposed to a *therapeutic* explanation.[1] A therapeutic explanation is a therapy—a method of treatment—that dissolves false consciousness and *thereby* emancipates the subject. Two clear instances of this kind of explanation are the Marxian analysis of capital as reified labor, which was intended to bring about the communist revolution by removing the ideological blindfold from the worker, and classic Freudian psychotherapeutic explanations, which are supposed to 'dissolve' neurosis by bringing repressed memories into the conscious mind. Therapeutic explanations rest on, but are not confined to, diagnostic explanations. A diagnostic explanation explains the causes of a crisis, and thus opens the way to confronting it, but it is not itself the means of emancipation. Nor does a diagnostic explanation or critique take a *substantive* evaluative stance with regard to the object of critique, although the questions raised within the analysis are determined by ideals that are taken to be fundamental (such as health in the case of medical diagnosis, and mutual understanding in the case of Habermas's theory). In other words, a diagnostic critique is not the same as a *moral* or *cultural* critique. In *The Theory of Communicative Action,* Habermas wished to construct a critique of societal rationalization that would reveal how the crises facing modern society may be explained as the result of a 'one sidedness' in the rationalization of Western societies. Although this critique ultimately is premised upon a commitment to the ideal of mutual understanding, it does not yet contain a commitment to or defense of particular substantive moral or cultural values against others.[2] Habermas's sociological hypothesis, which will be explained in Chapter 5, is that the processes in which culture is formed are threatened by the administrative and economic systems characteristic of modern societies. This hypothesis takes no substantive evaluative stand with regard to the particular cultural values that are threatened.

It is a feature of a critical theory of society in general, whether therapeutic or diagnostic, that it attempts a "self-clarification of the struggles and wishes of the age," in such a way as to guide those struggles.[3] Toward this end, it should also explain how a person, group, or society has come to be engaged regularly in practices that, in fact, are not in his, her, or its interest, as a result of some feature of that society. Another feature of critical theories of society is that they identify deep conflicts, or potentials for society-wide crises, inherent within the social, political, and economic institutions of modern capitalist societies. For example, Marx's theory of history attempts to explain the evolution of the institution of capitalism, an institution that is seen as conflicting with the interests of the working majority of early capitalist society. Because this conflict is ineradicable from capitalist societies in Marx's view, it would eventually lead to a major crisis—the revolution of the proletariat.

Often, Karl Marx is thought to be the first critical theorist, although not everyone agrees about what makes Marx's theory of history a critical theory. It is widely believed that the central critical moment of Marx's theory is the labor theory of value, which allows for the statement of the "contradictions" or manipulative illusions whose unmasking was to bring about the socialization of the means of production and a new kind of society.

Some scholars prefer to confine the use of the term *critical theorist* to the Frankfurt School theorists Theodor Adorno, Max Horkheimer, and Herbert Marcuse and their intellectual affiliates. Frankfurt School critical theory differs from Marx's theory of history principally in its evaluation of societal rationalization. For Marx, the evolving use of human rationality in improving our means of controlling nature contained an emancipatory potential, leading toward an efficient as well as liberated mode of production in the future communist society. The Frankfurt School, on the other hand, shared Weber's ambivalence toward the emancipatory potential of rationalization. In Weber's view, the more society becomes functionally organized and removed from tradition, the less freedom and meaningfulness are available to the individual.[4] Similarly, the Frankfurt School was concerned that rationalization entailed an ultimately senseless proliferation of bureaucratic offices, each issuing in further constraints on the individual. This absurd pursuit of perfect control leads, in the end, only to barbarism. "Enlightenment destroys itself."[5] The external constraints imposed by a rationalized society, then, are not its only regrettable feature; reason itself is inherently coercive, and its hold can be broken only by a flight into the irrational.[6]

Habermas does not share Adorno's pessimistic belief that a special form of barbarism is inherent to reason and modern society. As an aside, it is worthy of note that he also does not share the experiences of the early Frankfurt School theorists, who spent several years in exile in the United States during the Third Reich. Habermas, born in 1929, was a child when the Frankfurt School left Germany and later a youthful member of the Nazi Jugend (a children's organization concerned to instill German nationalism and loyalty to Nazi aims), learning of the Holocaust as a university student, after the surrender.

Habermas's conception of rationality—what he calls *communicative rationality*—more than anything else distinguishes his theory of societal evolution from the theories of Marx, Weber, and the Frankfurt School. Habermas rejects the equation (which he believes these individuals made) of rationality with what Weber called *Zweckrationalität* or "instrumental rationality." *Instrumental rationality* is defined as the rationality that governs the choice of means to given, usually material, ends. *Communicative rationality,* on the other hand, characterizes the activity of reflecting upon our background assumptions about the world, bringing our basic norms to the fore, to be questioned and negotiated. Instrumental rationality takes these background assumptions for granted, in the pursuit of new gains (cf. *TCA* I, 285–286). Habermas believes that the notion of instrumental rationality is insufficient to capture either the nature of *cultural evolution,* which is not governed merely by instrumental thinking, or the nature of economic and administrative systems, whose organization is too complex to be characterized as the product of instrumental planning. Rather, cultural evolution is a process fed by collective reflection on the whole range of values to which the society is committed. Hence it is Habermas's understanding of the nature of culture, and not a misguided desire for a society without conflict or dissent, that motivates his positioning of the ideal of mutual understanding at the center of his critical theory. On the other hand, economic and administrative systems in modern welfare states are characterized by *functional rationality,* which holds of these systems independently of the intentions of the instrumentally acting agents within them. Thus, the functional rationality of a system is decided on the basis of its ability to achieve goals such as economic and political stability, whereas the instrumental rationality of agents' actions is determined by their ability to maximize (those agents') utility. In summary, instrumental rationality explains neither the culture nor the behavior of the capitalist welfare state.

With Weber, Habermas rejects the Marxist determinist assumption that the instrumentally rational development of capitalist production determines not only the objective or institutional conditions, but also the subjective or ideological conditions, of societal change. Habermas believes that the social construction of social reality is part of the process of social change. Social reality is constructed through what Habermas calls *communicatively rational* action, or communication between participants attempting to reach a rational consensus. An understanding of societal evolution can be gained, in his view, by understanding how social reality is constructed through consensus building.

Communication , according to Habermas, is inherently oriented toward mutual understanding, and the standards that govern communication are therefore conditioned upon reaching mutual understanding and, ideally, rational consensus (*CES,* 3). Communicatively rational action, then, is action that conforms to these standards. There are three fundamental types of valid rational consensus, corresponding to three basic ways in which a communicative act can be claimed to be valid. In asserting a statement, one implicitly claims that the sentence stated is *true.* In stating a prescriptive norm, one claims that the norm is *normatively valid.* Finally, in expressing a subjective state, one is implicitly claiming to be *sincere* or truthful. Habermas calls truth, normative validity and sincerity the *validity claims.*[7] The validity claims are made in everyday acts of speaking. By asserting something, I make the claim that an assertion is true; in issuing a demand on moral grounds, I make the claim that a norm is justifiable, and in expressing my subjective point of view, that my expression is authentic. These validity claims are made in everyday acts of speaking. To be capable of communicatively rational action is to be well versed in the use and defense of validity claims. Communicative rationality, then, or the rationality of understanding oriented action, is an ability to produce rationally motivating justifications for validity claims.

The ability to raise validity claims, Habermas believes, is the basis of the social bond.[8] The act of raising a validity claim affirms the mutual commitment to standards of validity that make communication, and thus the social relationship possible. This mutual commitment enables one to recognize one's own and the other's respective places in an intersubjectively shared world; it enables each of us to agree on "where we stand" with respect to each other and with respect to an objective world of "states of affairs," an understanding of which we share. Now, it is the claim that the validity standards are the basis of the social bond, more than any other, which establishes the significance of Habermas's theory for sociology and for any theory of the evolution of social institutions. If the validity standards are the shared basis on which we negotiate our evolving social institutions and arrangements, as well as our shared understanding of the objective world, then they must be part of—indeed central to—the explanation of societal change.

Although Habermas rejects the Marxian and Weberian hypothesis that instrumental or "strategic" rationality is *central* to societal evolution, he does not deny that strategic rationality regulates individuals' interactions in the economy and in political decision making. Strategically rational action is constrained on two fronts: on the one hand by the values underlying communicative rationality (theoretical, ethical, cultural, and aesthetic values), and on the other hand by the functional, systemic requirements of the economic and adminstrative systems. This reevaluation of the place of strategic and functional rationality in the explanation of societal evolution is the chief distinguishing feature of Habermas's theory of societal rationalization, as opposed to other theories of societal rationalization and the more recent systems theories. For Habermas, it is not the degree to which a society has harnessed nature to produce goods that determines its degree of rationalization, but the degree to which the use of the validity claims have been developed in that society's communicative practices.

It may be unclear how a theory intended to describe the evolution of human rationality and the development of social institutions that results, could also be a critical theory. Furthermore, if there could be such a theory, it would seem to violate the basic scientific requirement of value freedom. A theory cannot both contain normative content—that is, be critical of society— and be a scientific explanation. In response to the first concern, the explanatory-descriptive and normative-critical aspects of Habermas's critical theory both are derived straightforwardly from the theory of communicative rationality. Any model of human rationality is a (descriptive) model of a normative structure. The hypothesis of a theory of societal rationalization, then, is that the norms of rationality, as described by the theory of rationality, are operative in history. That is, they figure centrally in the history of our institutions and practices, by setting the standards for the choices we make. But the same norms provide the foundation for a critique of society.

The second concern, a familiar one among American philosophers and social scientists, is trickier. Although Habermas's theory of societal rationalization is intended to explain, among other things, how values take shape within a culture, rather than to take up the cause of particular values, it nonetheless is true that his theory is deeply critical of the modern capitalist welfare state. The normative force or validity of this critical content stands squarely on the validity of the norms of communicative rationality. If human rationality is based on the norms that Habermas believes it is based upon, then the critical content of his theory of society is strong, for it is framed by those norms. However, many of Habermas's critics believe that the necessary conditions of communication cannot provide the foundation for the very strong normative content that he draws from them.[9] We shall return to this question in Chapters 3 and 4.

Habermas himself explains the intertwinement of explanatory and critical purposes in his theory in another way, which might be helpful here. According to Habermas's introduction to his critical theory of societal rationalization, the concept of communicative rationality is employed in three ways in its construction.[10] First, it answers the metatheoretical question; In what ways *can* action be rational? The answer provides the conceptual framework for Habermas's model of the evolution of *culture.* Culture is modeled within this framework as evolving in three increasingly differentiated "spheres" that correspond to each of the three validity claims. Historically, the idea of culture dividing into these three spheres derives from Kant's three faculties of reason: the theoretical sphere of science, the practical sphere of morality and law, and the aesthetic sphere. The distinctions drawn among these spheres reflect Weber's belief that each of these three cultural arenas possesses its own internal logic of development (*TCA* I, 159–164). According to Habermas, developments in each of these spheres are governed by the standards of validity (truth, normative validity, and expressive validity).

Second, the concept of communicative rationality is applied in the interpretation of culture: to grasp the cultural learning processes that lead to modern culture, the theorist is obliged, in effect, to engage in consensus-oriented communication with past and present cultures. He or she can understand them only by acknowledging and challenging their claims to validity (*TCA* I, 115–116). At this second level of involvement of the theory of communicative rationality in the theory of society, a critical dimension is introduced. The theorist's participation in a "dialogue" with the evolving culture is a two-way exchange, both listening to its lived crises and challenging it to identify and reflect on its normative and theoretical assumptions.

A third way in which the concept of communicative rationality enters into Habermas's theory is as the *object* of observation. The evolution of communicative rationality in society is observed, and hypotheses about the patterns in its emergence formulated. This level of involvement of the concept of communicative rationality is also central to the critical purpose of Habermas's theory. It is the pathological tendencies or distortions of the ideal of communicative rationality, in the actual historical unfolding of communicative rationality, that his theory is intended to diagnose.

Habermas's theory of societal rationalization is not a complete history of society: it is an analysis of history and exists only in the form of a rough outline of the processes that have governed the emergence of modern society. In a completed theory of societal rationalization, hypotheses about the course of development of communicative rationality would take a more specific form, similar to that of Jean Piaget's model of cognitive development, Lawrence Kohlberg's model of moral development, and George Herbert Mead's reconstruction of the evolution of communication. These models share the feature of being empirical reconstructive hypotheses—they attempt to follow, empirically, the development of abilities with highly complex internal structures. Habermas's own work thus far is more of a rational or analytic reconstruction of the necessary components of communicative ability. However, he has made forays in the direction of integrating this reconstruction with the theories of Piaget, Kohlberg, and Mead. Because the evolution of communicative ability is part of cultural development as well as a development experience by each individual, however, a full reconstruction of the history of communicative ability would recount the stages of learning of societies as a whole, as they gradually came to distinguish between claims of truth and right, right and beauty, and beauty and truth.

Thus far I have been concerned with introducing the idea of a critical theory of societal rationalization, the theory of communicative rationality on which this theory rests, and the way in which the theory of rationality is marshaled to construct the theory of societal rationalization. However, I have not yet introduced the actual critical hypothesis about modern society defended in this theory. Habermas believes that the modern capitalist welfare state is undergoing a process of "one-sided rationalization." To explain this hypothesis, it is necessary to return to the distinction among strategic, functional, and communicative rationality. As was remarked earlier, Habermas does not completely reject the view that strategic and functional rationality are part of the explanation of societal evolution, but he does believe that they are derivative of communicative rationality, both conceptually and historically. Only at a relatively recent stage in our history do we find that functional and communicative rationality begin to "uncouple," so that some activities are regulated by functional rationality and others by communicative rationality. According to Habermas, modern society is characterized by a rift between two "worlds," each with its own basis for thought, action, and organization. The one world, called the *lifeworld,* is still based upon the norms of communicative rationality, which have consensus as their aim. The other, called the *system,* is based on the demands of material production (as in Marx's theory of history). Habermas hypothesizes that the system increasingly tends to interfere with and distort the communicative activity in which the pursuit of knowledge and ethical understanding takes place.

The consequences of this bifurcation of rational action can be described from two perspectives, corresponding, not surprisingly, to the division between the system and the lifeworld. From the global, unengaged "noncommunicative" perspective of the system, the system's tendency to undermine the lifeworld results in system dysfunction, as the individuals entering into it are less and less prepared to accept the cultural presuppositions on which the system itself rests. For example, the system depends on individuals willing to sacrifice short-term gains for the sake of anticipated long-term gains. However, such willingness does not occur "naturally"; it is the product of an ethos. Unless this ethos prevails, fewer individuals will be prepared to make the kinds of sacrifices that our system demands.

From the engaged perspective of the lifeworld, the result of one-sided rationalization is a loss of autonomy and meaningful activity. This loss is real and not merely perceived; it cannot be answered with a "free" exercise of a will to give meaning to activity. As the system expands to meet the demands placed on it, it reorganizes or otherwise disrupts just those domains of activity in which freedom and meaning were to be founded. The critical claims of Habermas's theory, then, arise not only from the engaged perspective of the communicatively rational theorist in dialogue with the lifeworld, but also from the perspective of the observer of the functionally rational system in interaction with the lifeworld.

If Habermas's claims about the history of modern society are to hold up, then it is important that his critique of rationality be viable. For this reason, the following three chapters will be devoted to the arguments that he makes in support of it. Chapters 2 and 3 will describe Habermas's defense of his consensus theories of truth and normative correctness. The norms that govern argumentation concerning truth claims and argumentation concerning normative validity claims constitute the principal part of the norms that govern communication in general, or the norms of "universal pragmatics." Before turning to the theory of societal rationalization, the fourth chapter will explain the sincerity claim and Habermas's defense of his universal pragmatics as a whole.

CHAPTER 2

A Consensus Theory of Truth and Knowledge

Jürgen Habermas's consensus theory of truth is part of a general theory of communicative competence, a theory intended to answer the question: How is *mutual understanding between speakers* possible?[1] Habermas believes that mutual understanding is possible in virtue of the norms of communicative rationality, and that communicative competence in general just is the implicit knowledge of these norms. Those norms that concern making assertions, or more precisely, making *truth claims,* are the subject of this chapter.

Habermas's theory of communicative competence diverges at the outset from the more familiar theories of linguistic competence, such as that of Noam Chomsky, which are designed to answer the question, What knowledge must a speaker have to be able to speak and understand a *language?*[2] Habermas believes that an adequate account of our ability to learn and use language would have to take the phenomenon of mutual understanding as its fundamental object of explanation, rather than the speaker's understanding of a language. The obvious importance of mutual agreement in politics, science, morality, and personal relationships lends some weight to Habermas's conviction that this fragile phenomenon is the implicit *telos* of all communication and that communicative ability can be understood only with respect to it.[3]

Anyone who is fully capable of communicating in some language has at least an implicit grasp of a concept of truth. Not everyone is capable of putting his or her understanding of the concept into words, but every competent speaker is aware that one is held accountable for implying that certain utterances make true statements. The notion of truth possessed by a communicatively competent speaker is, according to Habermas, a consensus concept of truth (cf. *V*, 135–136). For a person possessing such a concept, the truth is what would be the outcome of a rational consensus achieved under ideal conditions. A rational consensus is one that all participants in the consensual procedure are rationally motivated to accept (*CES*, 3; *TCA* I, 287). Because rational motivation to accept the consensual position is a necessary condition of a rational consensus, such a consensus is never an "agreement for the sake of agreement." If this requirement is to be met, it is necesssary that the procedure be impartial, so that no relevant information that could have been included is excluded (as by excluding certain people from participating or by duress or misrepresentation; *TCA* I, 287). Thus Habermas believes that for a person to possess communicative competence, or, what comes to the same thing for him, for a person to be capable of reaching mutual agreement with others, that person must possess the consensual understanding of the meaning of the word 'truth'.

The Meaning of 'Truth'

Theories of truth fall into roughly five categories: correspondence theories, coherence theories, pragmatist theories, semantic theories, and redundancy theories.[4] At the outset, it should suffice to distinguish the first three from each other. Correspondence theories hold that true sentences "correspond" to, and are true in virtue of that correspondence with, some actual state of affairs in the world. Because the correspondence theory is extremely difficult to defend, although intuitively plausible, many contemporary philosophers have adopted coherence or pragmatist views of truth. A coherence theory of truth holds that those sentences are true which cohere with (entail, are entailed by, or are consistent with) our other beliefs. Habermas's consensus theory of truth is most aptly characterized as a pragmatist theory of truth. Like pragmatist theories, it asserts that the meaning of 'truth' must be given in terms of the means of vindicating claims about the truth of statements (or a truth criterion). Understanding the sense of 'truth', for the consensus theory and for pragmatist theories generally, is knowing what would constitute a decisive ground for affirming or disaffirming an asserted statement. Habermas believes that universal consensus under ideal conditions is the ground or criterion of correct truth claims, and that this criterion constitutes the meaning of 'truth' as the term is used in practice.[5] The truth, then, is defined by a consensus theory of truth as that which is agreed on under ideal conditions.

Habermas's consensus theory of truth derives its outlines from pragmatism—most notably that of Charles Saunders Peirce—and from speech act theory, especially from P. F. Strawson's views on truth. From Strawson, Habermas takes the argument that the truth predicate, its grammatical form notwithstanding, does not function in our language as a genuine predicate, but rather fulfills a special (nonpredicative) communicative function. For Habermas, this function is the raising of truth claims, an act that draws attention to the justifiability of the speaker's statement. From pragmatism, he adopts the pragmatist conviction that understanding the meaning of 'truth' rests on a conception of how truth claims are justified.

Some (most notably Russell) have argued that such theories of truth confuse the meanings of 'truth' and 'knowledge', and some definitions of truth (such as Alfred Tarski's) are intended to be neutral on the questions of how truth claims are justified and what constitutes a truth criterion.[6] True belief can be distinguished from justified true belief or knowledge. However, for Habermas as for pragmatists, this distinction is less significant than it is for Russell, as in Habermas's view we cannot speak of true belief without invoking the means for successfully justifying it, even though particular speakers may be unaware of those means. The reason is that we learn the concept of truth by applying it in communication, and in communication, it is applied in making an implied claim about our assertions; namely, that we are ready to back them up.

For Habermas, the meaning of 'truth' can be found, then, by looking at the use of the term in communication. The term is used for certain reasons, and understanding the reasons for which we employ the term is fundamental to an understanding of its meaning. The point of possessing a concept of truth, for Habermas, ultimately is a social one: the distinction between knowledge and ignorance is not made to satisfy the purposes of some disembodied ideal observer, but to fulfill the needs of a human community, one of whose most basic interests, Habermas believes, is the interest in achieving and maintaining a solidarity premised on mutual and rational agreement. A concept of truth divorced from this interest would be simply irrelevant.[7]

The raising of truth claims paradigmatically belongs to the making of assertions, and Habermas remarks that truth is to be understood with respect to this class of speech acts (*V*, 129). In other words, the meaning of 'truth' is to be found by describing the ability to perform an *act:* the act of raising a truth claim in making an assertion. Because the ability to raise a truth claim requires an awareness of and the ability to understand possible demands for its defense (as well as the point of making such demands), truth on this account is to be understood as a kind of warranted assertibility (*V*, 160).

Clearly, for Habermas, truth is not a mere device for semantic ascent (for stating of a sentence the material equivalence between it and another sentence in the metalanguage), as it has been for some philosophers in the analytic tradition who adhere to the semantic theory of truth.[8] Statements of the form "*p* is true" belong to a "higher order of discourse," but an order of discourse is defined with respect to communicative purposes rather than as a metalanguage, or a language of a higher logical type. Its definition belongs to a pragmatic theory of speech acts: a higher order of discourse is any discourse that is about discourse; for example, a discussion about a previous discussion or about a remark made by someone. A higher order of discourse is one in which the implicit truth claims of an object speech act (or a speech act in a lower order of discourse) can be made the explicit theme of a discussion and assessed for its justifiability. To state that *p* is true, then, is to focus on the means by which *p* could be justified and to commit oneself to their adequacy.

This holds, for Habermas, because of the meaning acquired by the expression 'is true' in its use in communication. The expression 'is true' is used to introduce the justifiability of a statement as the theme of a discussion. The ability to make the justifiability of a statement the theme of a discussion is one essential to the ability to communicate at all—what Habermas calls *communicative compe-*

tence. The meaning of 'truth', then, for Habermas derives from the role of the notion in achieving communicative purposes.

There are some parallels between the line of thought that Habermas follows and the "antirealist" position of the Oxford analytic philosopher Michael Dummett.[9] The understanding of truth that Dummett defends requires that for a sentence to be attributed with a truth value, there must be recognizable circumstances under which it could be shown or proven to be true or false. Truth for Dummett, then, is warranted assertibility. If realism entails that there could be truths that we could never know, or never have a means of justifying, then Dummett's (and Habermas's) views are clearly not compatible with realism.

Dummett and Habermas differ, however, in their intuitions about the point of possessing a truth predicate and in their notions of warranted assertibility. For both, communicative purposes account for the point of having a notion of truth, and the content of the notion is given by its role in achieving communicative purposes. But Habermas also believes, unlike Dummett, that all communicative purposes are instrumental in achieving the implicit *telos* of all communication—mutual agreement or consensus. Second, the warranted assertibility of a statement, for Habermas, obtains when and only when the statement is or would be the object of universal agreement. For Dummett, warranted assertibility is secured instead by provability or verifiability.

What, then, is the content of the idea of a rational consensus, the idea that is allegedly possessed or anticipated by any communicatively competent speaker? A rational consensus, a position to which the participants of the consensual group are rationally committed, is reached through discursive argumentation. The discussion comes to a close when all participants are rationally motivated, by the force of the better argument, to accept the outcome.

In place of a proof or verification procedure, Habermas defends a pragmatic 'logic' of discourse.[10] Discursive argumentation, the process required for the justification of a truth claim for a statement, follows a pragmatic discursive procedure that divides argumentation into three basic "modalities": the proof that a claim is absurd or impossible, the proof that a claim is necessarily true (the impossibility of the negation of a claim), and the justification of contingent statements. Habermas's interests do not extend to the first two, possibly because their role in social understanding is relatively minor.

The description of the justification procedure for contingent statements requires an account of reliable inference, or a 'logic of discourse.' A logic of discourse includes, but is not confined to, a set of truth-preserving operations on sentences. A discursive argumentation procedure also includes allowances and guidelines for the metatheoretical evaluation of the inferential procedures themselves and their suitability in a given context, as well as allowances for challenges to the adequacy of the theoretical language. The desire to allow for indefinitely many 'orders of discourse' or metatheopretical discussions motivates Habermas's choice of a pragmatic 'logic' of discursive argumentation, over a specific set of proof or verification procedures. These procedures themselves may, albeit rarely, come under criticism, and new proof procedures gain currency. The reliability of a procedure in turn is decided on the basis of its ability to motivate rational consensus.

A Problem

Habermas's theory of truth faces at least one major problem, which can be summarized as follows: Habermas's consensus theory claims to give an account of the meaning of 'truth' derived from its use in communication. However, the meaning of 'truth', in this account, is given in terms of a criterion that is *in principle* inapplicable, because the conditions specified by that criterion are unknowable. As a result, the consensus theory implies that we must be using the term 'true' either without any understanding of its meaning at all or in a mitigated (and disingenuous) sense. Before responding to this problem, it would be appropriate to explain what is meant by saying that the consensus theory defines truth in terms of an inapplicable criterion.

There is a simple way of showing why Habermas's consensus theory of truth cannot provide an effective criterion of correct truth claims. The reason that this holds is that there are no features of the discursive procedure that would distinguish a grounded (truth-claim vindicating) from an ungrounded consensus: the ideal conditions that define the rational consensual procedure do not specify when an apparent consensus is a grounded consensus, a consensus that would be reached "everywhere and always."

To say that *p* is true, Habermas writes, is that "a grounded consensus on the validity [truth] claim of the statement that *p*, is to be reached everywhere and always, whenever we enter into discourse" (*V*, 160). Now suppose there were an actual consensus that *p*. The problem is that nothing about such a consensus would preclude the occurrence of some other actual consensus that not-*p*. The truth claim that had been vindicated for the statement of *p* then is challenged, and a new discussion is necessary. Supposing that this discussion reaches a consensus, say that *p*, there still is nothing to prevent yet another consensus that not-*p*, and so on. Any actual consensus can be negated by some other consensus. The upshot of this is that a final consensus is *indistinguishable* from any other consensus, as its sole distinguishing feature—an eternal state of agreement—is not discoverable. Nothing about any actual agreement could indicate that it would be recognized as valid everywhere and *always*. The sorts of grounds and procedures that would rationally motivate an ultimate agreement are inaccessible.

Habermas's response has been to develop the consensus theory as an analysis of a regulative ideal that governs theoretical discourse, rather than as a truth criterion. This is not a severely disadvantageous concession, because it is not clear that a truth criterion of any kind is available. There is a limited sense in which it is possible to make sense of a consensus "criterion" of truth, not as a genuine criterion, but rather as an indicator of reliable beliefs. It involves the intuition that wide agreement on a given statement is an indicator of reliability in beliefs. This intuition also has been employed by prominent analytic philosophers of language and knowledge.[11]

One problem persists, however. If the meaning of 'truth' is to be given in terms of an intellectually *inaccessable* ideal (or what would seem to be the same, an incomprehensible ideal), then it would appear to follow that no speaker can have any notion of what is being claimed in the raising of truth claims! Depending on how it is further articulated, this could be a serious philosophical problem for a view like Habermas's, which claims to give an account of the meaning of 'truth' as it is understood by the communicatively competent speaker. At least one general positive response is open to Habermas: to apply the consensus concept of truth as a regulative ideal, it needs to be understood only as satisfiable by a state of *rationally grounded mutuality;* one need not have access to particular kinds of grounds or procedures that contain some guarantee of an ultimate consensus. To be sure, that agreement must be rationally motivated, but no preconditions are set upon just what kinds of grounds or procedures would succeed in bringing it about. The content of the notion of an ideal consensus, although it underspecifies what guarantees such a consensus, does specify that knowledge of the truth is, essentially, standing in a relation of mutuality to other persons about the world (rather than standing in a certain relation to the world, as it is for the correspondence theorist, or of discerning a relation between sentences and sentences, as it is for the coherence theorist). This suggestion draws on the conviction, often apparent in Habermas's writing, that a person who is not communicatively competent would not be capable of an orientation to the objective world, as an intersubjectively accessible world about which defensible claims can be made.

Mutual rational agreement is not, then, and should not be understood as a truth criterion, but rather an indicator of reliable beliefs, some of which, in the end, may turn out to be false. It is not possible to tell from the present consensual situation alone whether further developments will alter the consensus in the future. In recognition of these issues, Habermas has explicitly adopted a fallibilistic view of theoretical discourse and speaks of truth as an anticipated ideal.[12]

For Habermas, mutual rational agreement is not merely an indicator of reliable beliefs; it is also an end in itself, over and above the instrumental gains made available by expanded knowledge. Habermas believes that the anticipation of mutual agreement or consensus is a mainstay of the life of any social being and learning how to communicate, ultimately, means becoming capable of fulfillment as a rational member of a society. No account of communicative competence is adequate unless it acknowledges the fundamental importance of the interest in achieving mutual understanding— an interest that not only is necessary for a stable society and the best social relations, but that Habermas believes, we all possess by nature. Furthermore, the ability to communicate itself requires a commitment to the achievement of consensus and, specifically, the rational defensibility of truth claims, where truth claims are defensible if and only if they can be vindicated in the ideal speech situation. Therefore, although no actual consensus can be called an *ideal consensus,* the ideal is "anticipated" in the practices of any communicatively competent speaker. This anticipation is not empty of content, although this content consists in a particular kind of social relation, rather than in a particular kind of relation between beliefs and the world.

Habermas's consensus theory of truth competes with other philosophical theories of truth. Although with one or two exceptions, Habermas is less interested in defending this position vis-à-vis other philosophers of language and philosophers of knowledge than in developing it within his theory of societal rationalization, the importance of this understanding of truth to the latter project demands that it be philosophically well supported. This explains the great effort that Habermas has devoted to explaining and defending his consensus theory of truth and the general theory of which it is a part, the theory of communicative competence. In the following chapter, we shall look at Habermas's theory of normative justification, which constitutes another part of his theory of comunicative competence.

CHAPTER 3

A Consensus Theory of Normative Validity

Habermas's (1983) essay "Ethics of Discourse" opens with a recollection of the conviction, now familiar among philosophers, that the "project of the enlightenment, to ground a secularized, nonmetaphysical and nonreligious ethics, has failed."[1] For Habermas, this failure has less to do with the secular or antimetaphysical character of enlightenment ethics than with the direction taken by developments in ethical theory following the enlightenment, particularly those influenced by rational choice theory and by 'decisionism.' *Decisionism* is a term used primarily in the German-speaking world to denote a noncognitivist position, of which R. M. Hare (*Language of Morals* and *Freedom and Reason*) is taken as representative by Habermas.[2] Roughly, decisionism could be characterized as moderate value relativism. A decisionist position holds that although there are standards that moral judgments must meet, and rational criticism of moral judgments is therefore possible, the values on which choices of moral principles rest are part of a "way of life" and are not themselves subject to rational discussion.[3]

Habermas wished to counteract these developments with a theory of validity for ethical norms that also subjects the choice of values to rational discussion, while avoiding a return to metaphysical or transcendental foundations. He charged the influence of rational choice theory with having led to an unreflective use of goal-oriented or instrumental rationality, to the exclusion of reflection on our values and interests.[4] To the extent that the question, 'What may we and what may we not do, to satisfy our desires and preferences?' has been regarded as a fundamental question for ethics to answer, such reflective questions as, 'Are our values acceptable?' and 'What collective interests do we have?', in Habermas's opinion, have received less than satisfactory treatment. Although it is not obvious, the ends we pursue are shaped not in isolation from, but in interaction with, the people and cultural and social institutions around us. Habermas's defense of the consensus theory of normative validity is an attempt to show the meaningfulness of reflective questions about the shaping of our ends, as well as to account for the content of ethical norms by showing how normative validity claims can be justified.

Habermas's metaethical theory is a theory of justification for ethical norms that stands solidly in the Kantian tradition. The most important difference between Habermas's theory and Kant's *Grundlage* lies in their respective procedural definitions of acceptable norms. Habermas criticizes the nonconsensual or 'monological' character of the Kantian defense of ethical principles (*MCCA,* 65–67)). For Habermas, a valid norm must rest on consensually defined ends—ends that are identified as genuine common interests and express a "common will" (*MCCA,* 63). Only such interests can sustain the normative or binding force of ethical norms. The procedure for the vindication of normative validity claims and the procedure for the vindication of truth claims are quite similar: a norm is acceptable if it would be unanimously assented to in the ideal speech situation. In contrast, for Kant, ethical principles must meet the universalizability condition specified in the categorical imperative, a condition that can be met without an actual consensus. For this reason Habermas calls Kant's theory of normative validity *monological.*

With R. M. Hare, Habermas shares the conviction that it is possible to show that ethical norms, which contain 'ought' expressions, raise claims to universal validity, by giving a full account of the *meaning* of ought.[5] The meaning of 'ought', like the meaning of 'truth', in Habermas's view, can be discovered in the usage of the communicatively competent speaker. Any such speaker must, in virtue of being communicatively competent, be capable of recognizing and raising normative validity claims, and such claims inherently possess universal scope. Habermas argues that the universal scope of normative validity claims is entailed by the content of the norms that make communication possible: the norms of communicative rationality. In this chapter, we shall examine this argument, and its non-Kantian reliance on a consensual process of interest formation.

Normative validity claims are raised only indirectly in normal daily interaction, usually in the utterance of directives or grammatical imperatives. For example, in telling someone to shut the door, I am indirectly raising a normative validity claim for some norm or set of norms; such as the norm: it is not uncivil or inappropriate to request that someone perform simple tasks as a favor, so long as making such a request would not be disrespectful toward or inconvenient for that person, given his or her circumstances. When utterances that indirectly raise validity claims are challenged, the problematic norms are made explicit and the validity claim raised directly. If the validity of the norm is itself challenged, then argumentation—practical discourse—begins.

The discursive procedure that Habermas proposes for the vindication of normative validity claims is quite similar to the one that Hare proposes for the rational criticism and defense of moral judgments, with the exception that Habermas includes a stage for reflection on needs and interests. For Hare, a moral decision is justified by giving an account of the effects of the decision, the moral principles it observes, and the effects of observing those principles in all contexts. Any effect of an action that would be relevant to someone's interests or inclinations must be considered in the justification of the decision.[6]

For Habermas, the "casuistic evidence" brought in support of a norm includes the "consequences and side effects of applying the norm for the fulfillment of accepted needs" and interests.[7] The restriction of the evidence to *accepted* needs and interests means that statements about needs and interests are not taken at face value, but must pass collective critical reflection in the ideal speech situation. Thus the parallels to Hare's justificational procedure leave off where Habermas specifies that the interests which count as primary evidence for *ethical* norms must be *generalizable* interests—the interests of a "general" will, achieved in a consensual situation (*MCCA,* 63).

Habermas believes that individual's experiences and interests do not provide sufficient grounds for validity claims. Personal experiences and interests must be subjected to reflective and collective criticism and, through reflection, "transcended" or made intersubjective (*MCCA,* 67–68). Through theoretical discourse, private experiences are placed within a conceptual framework, understood, explained, and brought into accord with the world that others share. In a like manner, private interests are recognized as generalizable or acceptable interests through practical discourse. This implies that some statements about interests are unacceptable. Indeed, one of the implications of Habermas's consensus theory of normative correctness is that *anti*-social interests are not generalizable interests; in other words, they are founded on the denial of more basic and general interests, and such denials are incoherent. The discovery of generalizable and acceptable interests is the result of a collective effort—a process Habermas calls *discursive will formation.* If we are to understand what is unique about Habermas's "discourse ethics," we need to understand the way in which he believes that genuine generalized interests are formed. The following section will explain the process of discursive will formation, as it is envisioned by Habermas. First, a few remaining points of introduction should be made.

Habermas's philosophical view of the nature of ethical norms is sometimes identified with or likened to ethical cognitivism. Cognitivism in ethics is distinguished by its claim that ethical norms can be true or false. However, Habermas's theory of normative correctness claims not that ethical norms are true or false, but that they are normatively valid or invalid. Normative validity claims, and the competence required for the ability to raise them, are categorially distinct from theoretical or truth claims, because the former concern normative statements, which concern "the normative reality of what is intersubjectively recognized as a legitimate interpersonal relationship," and the latter descriptive statements, which concern "the external reality of what is supposed to be an existing state of affairs" (*CES,* 28). Valid norms are universally acceptable as choice constraining principles; true statements are universally acceptable as descriptions of states of affairs.

Second, not all norms must be shown to have universal validity, in Habermas's view. In other words, not all norms derive their normative force from consensually defined *generalizable* or universal interests. This is because not all the norms that figure in day-to-day social interaction are ethical norms. Although it may be argued that most social norms have some ethical content, not all social norms are ethical norms in their own right; for example, rules of etiquette or tactfulness, standards of "professionalism", the expectations of family members, friends, or neighbors for each other, and standards of affiliation within private associations. Habermas distinguishes nonethical social norms from ethical norms by distinguishing the procedures by which their validity would be vindicated. Because Habermas believes that valid ethical norms are universally valid, the procedure for vindicating the validity of an ethical norm is a procedure for showing it to be universally acceptable. A validity claim for a nonethical social norm would be vindicated by the consensus of a group sharing some set of interests or characteristics; it would not be necessary to show that the norm held for any larger group (*MCCA*, 104). More will be said in the following chapter, on the validation of nonethical norms.

Discursive Will Formation and Need Interpretation

The participants in the ideal speech situation need to know what are their needs and interests, which of them have higher priority, and how they may be balanced against each other, if the participants are to decide whether a given norm is valid or not. Needs and interests play the role of "evidence" in the determination of valid norms in the ideal speech situation. Norms are agreed to be correct or incorrect on the basis of their foreseeable consequences for the needs and interests of all concerned, for "norms regulate the legitimate opportunities for the satisfaction of needs" and interests (*V*, 172).

Those needs and interests of greatest importance to the defense of ethical norms are ***universal*** or ***generalizable*** needs and interests, as an ethical norm could be universally valid only if it could derive its validity from common interests. A norm cannot be universally valid if it represents partial interests (*V*, 172–173). However, it is important to point out that when Habermas speaks of universal or "generalizable" interests, he is not referring to interests that are general merely in the sense that everyone has them (such as the interest in being adequately nourished). What Habermas calls ***generalizable interests*** belong to a smaller, and more strongly specified, class of interests: interests that are discovered in the context of, and which sustain, a 'general will.' One possible way of defining such interests, although it is not Habermas's, might be to define them as those interests it is (at least as discovered in the ideal speech situation) in everyone's interest that everyone should have. Social welfare and personal liberty provide likely examples of such interests. Ethical norms, which proscribe the ethically impermissable exercise of nongeneralizable interests (and allow the permissible exercise thereof), derive their validity from their ability to represent generalizable interests.

Habermas claims that generalizable interests are discovered, and yet at the same time formed, in a consensual situation.[8] They are interests that we discover only as social beings, and only through reflective dialogue. There are some unanswered questions about the difference between claims about generalizable interests and claims about nongeneralizable interests. In general, claims about interests raise "sincerity" or "expressive-aesthetic" claims rather than truth claims. A sincerity claim is a claim that one has spoken honestly and, unlike truth or normative validity claims, is not redeemable through rational consensus.[9] Because generalizable interests are consensual, it would seem that statements about general interests raise ***discursively redeemable*** validity claims that can be vindicated only through rational consensus; in other words, that they raise ***truth*** claims. Claims about the interests that justify ethical norms must be recognized as valid in a rational consensus, but they could not, if all claims about interests were merely 'disclosures of subjectivity.' This feature of generalizable interests clearly divides them from personal and nongeneralizable cultural values, whose expressions raise no truth claims, but rather the third kind of validity claim, that of sincerity.

Although the status of claims about generalizable interests is somewhat unclear, the distinction between generalizable interests and nongeneralizable interests or values clearly is essential for Habermas's ethical theory, as the former, but not the latter, must be capable of commanding universal recognition, apart from membership in particular communities and cultures (*MCCA,* 104). On the other hand, Habermas appears to wish to lend particular cultural values, or ideas of the 'good life,' at least a marginal role in the design of ethical norms, remarking that such values at least can be *candidates* for embodiment in those norms (*MCCA,* 104).

The interpretation and expression of nonuniversal needs, desires, and values clearly are an important part of self-realization and cultural life. These are the values that give content to our understanding of the 'good life,' as opposed to the 'just' life, within our respective cultures and subcultures.[10] These values also provide the ground for nonethical social norms, which include everything from norms of proper conduct and civility to norms governing friendship, partnership, marriage, and family. It is clear that the nongeneralizable values include many that are embodied in what is left, in the modern era, of tradition. Habermas shares with Max Weber the concern that the modern era is threatened with the loss of values of this kind (and a 'loss of meaning' as a result) as the social activities in which they emerge and are defined disappear.

Unfortunately, Habermas has not spoken as clearly about the role of nongeneralizable interests, or social and cultural values, in society as he has about that of generalizable interests, in the justification of ethical norms. Where some cultural values fall into the 'value sphere' of the expressive and aesthetic, it is unclear where, for Habermas, social values (such as the value of the 'traditional family' or, alternatively, of the 'women's community') have a place in the formation of culture and society. This has led Habermas, in my view, to lump various kinds of social activism and experimentation together with the subjective exploration he imagines as corresponding to the expressive-aesthetic region of culture.[11] I will return to the role of expressive-aesthetic (sincerity) claims, which are raised in the expression of personal desires and values, in the discussion of communicative rationality in Chapter 4.

Habermas also has been criticized for the insensitivity of his theory of normative validity to cultural difference.[12] It is important that any ethical theory recognize that there may be nonuniversal forms of relationship and practices that should not be automatically overridden, in every case, by prima facie universal norms. At the same time, Habermas makes no claim that "we" have a privileged route to universal norms: clearly, any differences, including those deriving from culture, must be recognized in the ideal speech situation. Moreover, Habermas agrees that the nonuniversal values that take shape within a given culture are not ethically irrelevant, and that it is possible to subject them to rational criticism. Nonetheless, in a conservative reading of Habermas, claims about such values (including nonuniversal social, personal, and aesthetic values) are not understood as capable of *discursive validation* and for this reason do not play any kind of direct role in the justification of universal ethical norms.[13]

Discursive will formation, or the discovery of genuinely generalizable interests, occurs as a result of an interactive process that Habermas calls *need interpretation.* Let us consider how a person knows that he or she has certain needs or interests, and whether people have those needs and interests they say they have. Undoubtedly, the existence of certain easily definable general needs is unquestionable, such as those required for basic health, security, and stability. These, however, are only a few of our basic needs and interests. Habermas argues that our understanding of all our needs depends on the adequacy our interpretive framework: "The capacity for an argument to bring about mutual agreement stands upon the assumption that that conceptual system is adequate, within whose bounds the . . . generally accepted needs that are brought in support [of a norm] are interpreted. . . . The selected conceptual system must allow that and only that interpretation of needs, in which the participants make transparent and recognize their inner nature—what they truly want" (*V,* 173).

At least two immediate and obvious objections might be raised against this position. First, the adequacy of the conceptual scheme and the genuineness of the interpretation of needs are interdefined, without any independent means of recognizing when one or the other has been achieved. Habermas's answer to the question of how genuine common interests are discovered sounds unavoidably circular: the conceptually adequate language of need interpretation is that which we agree to be the right one (because it makes our inner natures transparent, we recognize what we truly want by using it, and so forth). A second problem is that this process appears to remove the question of what one's interests are from the individual, since his or her acknowledgment of certain needs is neither a necessary nor sufficient condition for actually having them. People can have certain needs, according to this picture, without agreeing that they do, or they can agree to having needs that they do not have; their agreement is valid only when they have interpreted their needs genuinely, that is within an adequate conceptual system.

Although Habermas does not address these particular issues, it is possible to reconstruct possible responses to them. First, the purpose of need interpretation may not be as much to overcome self-deception or reveal some hidden genuine interest, as it is to recognize and extend the public character of the articulation of basic common needs and interests. The lack of public discourse and participation by all concerned often emerges in Habermas's work as a deeper problem in the modern era than ideologically distorted thinking or false consciousness. An adequate interpretive framework then, is not necessarily guaranteed to allow the expression of 'true' human interests for all time, but is one that reflects the participation of all concerned.[14] Second, it is often overlooked that the ideal speech situation serves the individual well—arguably better than a representative democracy. Many of Habermas's readers seem to have the impression that the ideal speech situation is potentially paternalistic, as though someone else's consensus is somehow forced on the individual participants. But a genuine consensual position must command the uncoerced assent of all participants. No one is entitled by the consensus theory to discount another's position, and everyone is free to make up his or her own mind. This arrangement extends significant freedoms and responsibilities to each individual subject. Habermas does not want to prejudge the question of what are our true 'generally acceptable' interests, believing that this is a question for all of us to decide.

It is true that Habermas also wishes to propose that we already do have knowledge of at least some of our true—and generalizable—interests. One of these interests is the interest in achieving mutuality. The interest in mutuality, Habermas thinks, must be universal, because even imperfect communication could not succeed unless we had it. Habermas attempts to support this claim in his general theory of communicative competence, which we shall discuss in the following chapter. Once the existence of this interest is established, other interests can be derived from our knowledge of the conditions that would have to obtain for perfect understanding and agreement. For example, Habermas might say that, because the use of force is a coercive and not a rational means of influencing behavior, it must be opposed to the interest in achieving mutuality; and it therefore contradicts the basis of communicative action. Now, if we all, insofar as we are communicatively competent participants, have an interest in achieving mutual agreement on public affairs, then barring extraordinary circumstances, we have a common interest in keeping the use of force to a minimum in accomplishing public tasks. Similar arguments could be made in regard to any interest or need that cannot be shown to be compatible with the interest in achieving mutual understanding.

There are at least some remote parallels between this way of determining our true interests and Kant's procedure for deriving the ethical constraints on the will from the nature of the rational subject.[15] For Kant, the rational subject must recognize that the highest good is the good will (in virtue of its capacity to give itself its own moral law), and the moral law, which enjoins respect for all who possess this capacity, follows. Here, the role played by the nature of rationality in Kant's *Groundwork* is played by the conditions on the ideal speech situation (which, as should become more apparent, Habermas believes to be definitive of rationality in its fullest sense); and our true generalizable interests turn out to be the values that one must be committed to, if one is to be communicatively competent. However, where Kant's procedure involves splitting off the (rational) will from contingent human interests, Habermas's procedure attempts to integrate them. To the extent that our generalizable interests can nonetheless be derived from a priori assumptions (such as that to be communicatively competent is to be interested in mutuality), the attempt to introduce contingent human interests into Kantian ethics would appear to be less than sincere.[16] In the following section, however, another reading of Habermas's intentions will be considered: though generalizable interests must be compatible with the ideal of mutuality, this ideal does not exhaust the content of those interests.

Generalizable Interests and the Principle of Universalization

The principal formal constraint on the vindication of normative validity claims in practical discourse is the principle of universalization. In moral argumentation, such a fundamental formal constraint—a constraint that all ethical norms must fulfill—amounts to what Kant called a *principle of morality.* For Kant, the principle of morality is the categorical imperative. Habermas's principle of morality also functions as a 'bridge principle', one that makes use of knowledge about interests and the consequences of policies and actions for the fulfillment of needs and interests to decide on the validity of ethical norms.

The fundamental principle of morality, Habermas writes in "Discourse Ethics," "should be so formulated that all norms which cannot be acknowledged by all of those possibly concerned are excluded as invalid. The bridge principle which makes rational consensus possible should, therefore, ensure that only those norms which express a *general will* are acknowledged as valid: they must be qualified, as Kant said, for the status of a 'general law'" (*MCCA, MH,* 63). Nonetheless, he criticizes the categorical imperative, because it does not countenance the interests of actual persons, but only hypothetical persons imagined by the moral subject. Similarly, he criticizes Rawls for aggregating individual wills and failing to develop the idea of a "general will"—one that wills in accordance with generalizable interests (*MCCA,* 65–67).[17] Procedures that fail to countenance a general will Habermas calls *monological.*

A principle of universalizability may take several forms. One form quite easily fulfilled specifies only that a norm contain no proper names or indexical terms (anything that functions like an individual constant in first-order logic). Although this reading of the principle may be too restrictive in some discussions of nonmoral norms (for example norms with restricted scope of application), it is not sufficiently restrictive as a principle of morality, because imperatives that are obviously immoral may also be derived from it. For example, "Inferior people ought to be exterminated" contains no proper names or references to particular circumstances, though it is conceivable that someone might be able to will that this maxim were universal. The 'Golden Rule' reading comes closer to our moral intuitions, but still does not suffice to capture impartiality. Although one may *consistently* will that every person in a like situation do some act *x,* this does not itself imply that all others concerned also must will that every person in a like position do *x.* This second condition (that everyone will the universalization of the same maxim), Habermas argues, cannot be fulfilled by a 'monological' principle. "The intuition expressed in the idea of the generalizability of maxims means something more than this, namely, that valid norms must *deserve* recognition by *all* concerned. It is not sufficient, therefore, for *one* person to test whether he can will the adoption of a contested norm" (*MCCA,* 65).

At best, Habermas argues, monological universalization serves some concerned; given the limitations of individual persons, it cannot serve all. Habermas's claim that a consensual (nonmonological) universalization is possible turns on the existence of generalizable interests. If there are generalizable interests, as Habermas believes, then a maxim specifying only that I must be able to will that all others do as I do must fail as genuine universality, as nothing stated in the maxim guarantees that my will answers to those generalizable interests. If there are generalizable interests, then a monological principle, in all likelihood, would be insufficient for universalization.

On the other hand, if these generalizable interests are not contingently discovered in actual consensus but, rather, are rational interests (discovered by reason), as Habermas also seems to imply, then would it not be possible to apply the principle of universalization as a monological but reflective principle? It is a premise of the theory of communicative action that social actions (actions whose rationale and ends are not indifferent to the responses, expectations, and ends of other agents) are paradigmatically communicative and, as such, are oriented toward coming to a mutual understanding (see Chapter 4). The argument for this premise is not that it has been accepted in an actual consensual situation, but rather that an interest in consensus is a 'condition of the possibility' of any communication at all. Habermas's supporting argument for his contention that consensus is a generalizable interest is a 'monological' one. Furthermore, it seems that other generalizable interests could be derived from this one, because any interests that are incompatible with consensus would have to be ruled out. But is this not inconsistent with Habermas's claim that generalizable interests are "discovered" in the ideal speech situation?

One could suggest that the value of rational consensus itself is a contingent value, discovered only in the course of our efforts at communication. Holwever, this does not appear to be Habermas's intent, given his argument that this interest is inherent to all communication. Its status is that of a condition of the possibility of other interests: the value of consensus must be recognized, if the consensually determined interests of a society are to be met at all. But this entails no constraints on *when* or *what* consensus about the other generalizable interests must be reached. The conditions of the ideal speech situation provide formal contraints on acceptable interests, but are not sufficient for their discovery. Generalizable interests are not discovered merely by "deriving" them from the conditions of the ideal speech situation. For this it is necessary to address the actual concerns of the participants.

Habermas gives few suggestions for what the notion of a general will might entail. A rare glimpse occurs in *Communication and the Evolution of Society:* "The 'pursuit of happiness' might one day mean something different—for example, not accumulating material objects of which one disposes privately, but bringing about social relations in which mutuality predominates and satisfaction does not mean the triumph of one over the repressed needs of another" (*CES*, 199).

Habermas's criticism of the Kantian procedure for normative justification indicates a shift, also visible in this passage, in the notion of autonomy from a radical autonomy of the individual will to an autonomy that is found only where it is shared and that increases only when the gains are shared. At the very least, commitment to autonomy in this sense would entail the abolition of coercive institutions and the establishment and maintainance of common support systems.

Steven Lukes objects: "The idea seems to be that there will be an endogenous change of preferences on the part of social actors.... But why should one suppose such a moral change to be either possible, necessary or desirable... [or] that such a form of life... is uniquely capable of justification?"[18] In response to this objection it is important to recall that Habermas's recommendations take the form of very general constraints: a justifiable form of life must be free of distorted communication or coercion. All in all, he is not urging an endogeneous change in *preferences,* or the necessity or desirability of moral change, but a change in the means of determining what should be regarded as the "preferences of the people" and an expansion of the options beyond consumer goods and political privileges. The possibility of moral change has been demonstrated by history—it was once thought to be morally permissable in this country to own slaves, for example.

Justifying the Principle of Universalization

Habermas's argument in support of the consensual (nonmonological) universalization principle derives much of its inspiration from Karl-Otto Apel's work on a theory of transcendental pragmatics.[19] The very idea of supporting a principle of morality with a theory of pragmatics, a theory about how speakers employ language to make utterances, may seem odd. Recall that for Habermas, the pragmatic rules included in communicative competence, and most importantly, the rules governing the use of validity claims, just are norms of (communicative) rationality, including practical rationality. Habermas, however, attempts to avoid Apel's transcendental claims, defending the generalizations of universal pragmatics as contingent universal generalizations. As contingent generalizations about our speech acts, they are open to empirical corroboration and falsification.

In "Discourse Ethics," where the universalization principle is given its clearest and most extensive defense, the argument is conceived as a reply to the skeptical position that normative correctness, and specifically a principle of universalization, cannot be grounded.[20] As an argumentative device, Habermas introduces Apel's concept of a *performative contradiction.*[21] Apel himself borrowed the idea of such a 'pragmatic contradiction' from G. E. Moore.[22] A performative contradiction is similar in structure to a 'Moore sentence,' such as, for example, the sentence "There is a goldfinch in the yard but I don't believe that there is a goldfinch in the yard." A performative contradiction obtains when an assertion presupposes a noncontingent assumption (in this case, "If I sincerely assert that there is a goldfinch in the yard, then I believe that there is a goldfinch in the yard") that contradicts the asserted statement. Suppose the skeptic's objection to the justifiability of the universalization principle is formulated in the following way: "It is not possible to ground the universality of any norm." Habermas argues that the skeptic puts himself or herself in the position of committing a performative contradiction, for the skeptic presupposes, in making this assertion, the universal validity of at least those norms of rationality that are necessary to understand his or her own objection.

The argument contains a positive reply to the skeptic as well. If participation in argumentation can be shown to presuppose acceptance of certain universal rules of argumentation, and if the principle of universalization could be derived from these rules, then the principle of universalization could be shown to be universally presupposed: "Thus the necessary justification of the proposed moral principle could take the following form: every argumentation, regardless of the context in which it occurs, rests on pragmatic presuppositions from whose propositional content the principle of universalism (*U*) can be derived" (*MCCA,* 82). The resulting derivation would bear some resemblances to a transcendental argument, although Habermas wants to avoid going so far as to claim that the argument will provide an 'ultimate ground' (in the transcendental sense) for the principle of morality, something that Apel does claim. Habermas indicates that confirmation for the basic assumptions of discourse ethics will be empirical rather than analytic in nature (*MCCA,* 98). Habermas speaks of the 'reconstruction of universal presuppositions' rather than of transcendental argumentation and 'universal presuppositions of participation in communication' rather than of a communicative 'a priori.'

Habermas wants to show that, if a person participates in communication, that person presupposes the validity of not just some set of norms, but a particular set of universal norms, without whose acceptance communication would not be possible. As a premise we are to take the noncontingent fact that any one of us participating in this discussion, including the skeptic, is a participant in discourse. Lest the reader sense an impending *petitio principii* (question begging argument), it is important here only that discourse be understood as purposive action pertaining to a validity claim. That is, participating in discourse means seeking to succeed in doing something such as to convince, refute, arrive at a conclusion, and so on. Following the transcendental line of inquiry, one now asks, What must be so that this noncontingent fact is possible? Habermas claims that there are several *universal* conditions of the possibility of participation in discourse.

The next step in his argument, then, is the derivation of the principle of universalization from these 'presuppositions' or 'pragmatic universals' of all communication. Habermas states three exemplary pragmatic universals that "come close to implying" the principle:

- Any and every subject capable of speech and [social] action may take part in discourse.
- Any participant may problematize an assertion,
  Any participant may introduce any assertion into discourse.
  Any participant may express his [or her] position, wishes, and needs.
- No participant may be hindered, through coercion internal or external to the speech situation, in perceiving his [or her] hereby established rights.[23]

Anyone who acknowledges these rules of discourse, that is, anyone who "seriously attempts to vindicate a normative validity claim discursively," must also, at least implicitly, acknowledge the universalization principle, whose content amounts to the same as that of the rules: "a contested norm cannot meet with the consent of the participants in a practical discourse unless (*U*) holds, that is, unless all affected can *freely* accept the consequences and the side effects that the *general* observance of a controversial norm can be expected to have for the satisfaction of the interests of *each individual*" (*MCCA,* 93). If this can be derived from the rules of discourse, certainly the basic principle of discourse ethics itself is not far behind: "Only those norms can claim to be valid that meet (or could meet) with the approval of all affected in their capacity as participants in practical discourse" (*MCCA,* 93).

Our skeptic may respond in a number of ways, according to Habermas. First, she or he may deny that such reconstructions of pretheoretical competence or knowledge in general are defensible or genuine. This objection is not specific to moral skepticism and concerns several theories in linguistics and cognitive psychology. I will address this issue in the next chapter. Second, she or he may deny that the particular rules of discourse that Habermas names are genuine presuppositions or conditions of participation in discourse. Third, the skeptic may deny that the principle of universalization, so derived, is binding upon her or him as an agent. Habermas believes that both of the latter objections can be successfully countered. One might want to add a fourth objection: the argument sometimes uses interchangeably the 'a priori' and overriding interest in achieving mutual understanding as universal, and the knowledge that a speaker must have to be able to communicate (that is, as though 'serious' discourse is always discourse toward this end). Although Habermas claims that any communicatively competent speaker possesses both, the notion of communicative competence does not necessarily entail certain interests—this claim would have to be supported independently.

According to Habermas, particular rules of discourse, such as the ones just cited, can be shown to be *without alternative,* which is neither to claim that they are a priori nor to say that they may be genuinely grounded. Habermas denies that reconstructions of communicative competence may be verified directly. "The *certainty* with which we put our knowledge of rules into practice, does not extend to the *truth* of proposed reconstructions of presuppositions hypothesized to be general, for we have to put our reconstructions up for discussion in the same way in which the logician or the linguist, for example, presents his theoretical descriptions [of our logical or linguistic competences]" (*MCCA,* 97). However, it is possible to assemble indirect corroboration from psychological investigation of moral and communicative competence and its development. This possibility will be discussed in the following chapter. The other possibility is to show that (at least some of) the rules are without alternative—that flouting them draws one into a performative contradiction, whatever else one does. To the objection that the skeptic has no reason to regard the principle of universalization, so derived, as binding, Habermas replies that such a position implies an "empty, wordless" withdrawal from communicative interaction—a possible choice, but an unattractive one. The skeptic may refuse to reflect on these common features of social life, but a full denial of them would be a completely imaginary achievement, itself incomplete because such a life, in fact, is not imaginable. Such a skeptical response would be "an empty, a wordless, demonstration of arbitrary refusal." The skeptic has been driven into a corner, and Habermas has erected a formidable metaethical edifice on the assumption that we all share an interest in coming to mutual understanding, which overrides all other interests.

Albrecht Wellmer and Seyla Benhabib (independently) have raised powerful objections to this argument, at least parts of which must be mentioned, although it will not be possible to do their arguments full justice here.[24] Wellmer argues that the universalizability principle does not follow from the norms that constitute the ideal speech situation on the grounds that the norms of argumentation do not obligate us to enter into argumentation except under certain special conditions (that is, when the argument in question is relevant to our own convictions). The reason is that there is an important difference between the requirements of *rationality* and those of *morality:*

> The obligations of rationality concern themselves with the recognition of arguments, the obligations of morality with the recognition of persons. It is a requirement of rationality that I acknowledge the argument of an enemy, when it is good; it is a moral requirement to let those people speak who don't yet have good arguments. In summary: the obligations of rationality are concerned with arguments, without regard to persons, and moral obligations are concerned with persons without regard to their arguments. . . . only from an imaginary "ultimate point of view" of an ideal community of communication can it appear as though both [types of obligations] ultimately coincide.[25]

The point of this argument is that, although you may be obligated to listen to and take seriously arguments that pertain to a position you already have, you are not obligated *by the norms of rationality* to pursue a consensus on ethical norms with anyone and everyone on matters on which, as of yet, you take no position. Whether or not this objection is successful depends on whether participants in argumentation are committed to some ideal consensual position or rather, less strongly, merely to recognizing relevant objections and alternatives to given positions. In the following chapter, we will look at Habermas's argument that strong commitments to mutual understanding (and, in a strong interpretation of Habermas, to consensus) are made by participants in discourse.

It often has been suggested that Habermas's discourse ethics shares the least attractive feature of Kantian ethics; namely, its abstraction and disregard for contingent circumstances and special relationships. Seyla Benhabib makes a very strong case for this view. She argues that the universalizability principle does not follow from the norms of communicative competence without morally significant additional assumptions that are likely to be unacceptable to some, violating the requirement that the universalizability principle be accepted univocally. For example, if the requirement of rational discourse that "every agent capable of speech and action can participate in discourse" is taken literally, then communities whose moral intuitions are particularistic would violate this requirement. For Habermas's argument to follow, he would need to introudce the assumption that there are no (valid) particularistic moral intuitions. But those who have such intuitions would surely disagree. Moreover, the rules of discourse exclude those who cannot speak (children, animals). If so, then these rules contain "commitments of a moral philosophy" that "cherishes universalism" and includes only "responsible, equal adults" in its moral community.[26] Furthermore, if only certain kinds of people can enter into discourse, then the range of that discourse is limited as well.

In "Moralität und Sittlichkeit," Habermas addresses Hegel's objections to Kant's 'formalism' and 'abstract universalism,' which inspired much of Benhabib's argument.[27] Habermas reminds us of the historical origins of enlightenment ethics, pointing to the necessity for a formal procedural and universalizable (impartial) ethics in modern societies, which recognize the vulnerability of the individual with respect to potential or actual coercive power. Universalistic assumptions are present wherever there is condemnation of oppression and injustice. With regard to the imputation of formalism, he emphasizes that "the content that is tested by a moral principle is generated not by the philosopher but by real life."[28] As a consequence (and as was mentioned earlier), although the good life is defined, in part, independently of ethical values, that definition will come to be reflected in ethical principles. The more diverse the participants of discourse become, the more important becomes the stage of practical and aesthetic discourse that Habermas calls ***need interpretation,*** which raises the third validity claim, the sincerity claim, for expressions of particular needs and interests, because only very few needs and interests are generalizable and the role of nongeneralizable interests in any full conception of the 'good life' is substantial. This nature of aesthetic-cultural values will be further explored in the following chapter.

One final note should be made here concerning normative validity claims that pertain to societal and institutional organization and functioning. These are called ***legitimacy claims,*** and they constitute a special class of normative validity claims. Legitimacy claims are discursively redeemable validity claims (like all other normative validity claims) that are vindicated only through grounded consensus. They are raised implicitly by the very existence and ongoing activity of social organizations and institutions, and they are raised explicitly when challenged by the public. The procedure for vindicating legitimacy claims is the same as that for vindicating other normative validity claims: practical discourse. Habermas is particularly concerned to emphasize this latter point, as many are inclined to mistake ***legality*** or ***constitutionality*** alone for legitimacy.[29]

Habermas, unlike Rawls, does not attempt to derive specific principles of institutional legitimacy from the ideal speech situation or ideal precontractual situation. As we have seen, Habermas is opposed to the use of hypothetical persons in deriving norms, and he believes that the collective decisions of actual persons can be their only source. It is not the role of a critique of practical rationality, then, in Habermas's view, to determine substantive normative principles. Indeed, his analysis of the "dysfunctions" of the modern capitalist welfare state, which we will look at in Chapter 4, is not only (intended to be) ethically neutral, it is nonnormative and not intended to draw on any substantive conceptions of just institutions. However, the analysis identifies features of modern society that indirectly make themselves apparent, at the level of human experience, as failures of institutional legitimacy.

CHAPTER 4

The Theory of Communicative Competence

The previous two chapters have been devoted to two of the three validity claims that, as Habermas argues, make communication possible. There is a third validity claim, the sincerity or 'aesthetic-expressive' claim, which concerns the ability to express one's own subjectivity. The role of this validity claim in Habermas's theory of rationality and theory of societal rationalization is less clear, and possibly less important, than those of the first two validity claims. This question shall be raised in the first section of this chapter, the remainder of which explores the structure of all consensus-oriented action.

Aesthetic-Expressive Rationality

The discussions of theoretical rationality and practical rationality in Habermas's work, at least until the latter 1980s, have tended to overshadow the relatively brief and scattered references to the rationality of truthful self-expression and aesthetic expression. As a result, the role of aesthetic-expressive claims in the totality of our actions is less sharply focused in Habermas's work than are those of the other two validity claims. The aesthetic-expressive claim is first introduced along with the other validity claims in "Vorlesungen zu einer sprachtheoretischen Grundlegung der Soziologie" (1970–1971) as an offer of reliability or trustworthiness, rather than as a claim to aesthetic authenticity. This claim was first called the *truthfulness* or *sincerity claim* (*Wahrhaftigkeitsanspruch, V,* 110), and the function of expressive speech was described as the "disclosure of the speaker's subjectivity" (*CES,* 68) and the basis of "dramaturgical" or self-expressive action (*TCA* I, 326ff). This characterization of expressive action coheres well with the theory of speech acts within which it first appears. It is not immediately evident, however, that the norms of truthful self-disclosure can double as norms of aesthetic rationality or that sincere self-expression and aesthetic expression are the same thing. Indeed, when the truthfulness claim was first introduced, Habermas did not seem interested in the possibility that a form of *discourse* might correspond to this validity claim. Habermas has not changed his view that sincerity or aesthetic validity claims are not "discursively redeemable," but he now speaks freely of "aesthetic rationality" and "aesthetic discourse."

Another source of unclarity is the fact that Habermas has never been entirely clear as to what role aesthetic-expressive rationality is supposed to play with respect to communicative rationality as a whole. Habermas's use of the distinction between three value spheres—scientific-technical, moral-legal, and aesthetic-cultural—and his insistence that ethical values are "generalizable" or universal, strongly suggest that aesthetic and "cultural" values are distinct from those that underlie ethical decisions. On the other hand, Habermas has warned against treating the value spheres narrowly, risking 'moralism,' 'aestheticism,' and 'objectivism'.[1] Each of the three types of discourse provides cultural ballast for the discussion of issues within any one type of discourse. Aesthetic reason, moreover, may play a special unifying role with respect to all three types of discourse. He also appears to think that aesthetic-cultural values are involved in articulating the 'good life' (as opposed to 'the just life' (*das Gerechte*); see *MCCA,* 201).

Most of the clues to Habermas's concept of the aesthetic-expressive claim and the knowledge or discourse with which it is concerned come from brief passages such as the following:[2] "Expressive knowledge can be explicated in terms of those values that underlie need interpretations, the interpretations of desires and emotional attitudes. Value standards are dependent in turn on innovations in the domain of evaluative expressions. These are reflected in an exemplary manner in works of art" (*TCA,* 334). In this passage, Habermas's reasons for speaking of the truthfulness claim as the validity basis for "aesthetic-practical" knowledge emerge. Habermas casts art as the exemplary forum for the expression and exploration of alternative nonethical values. Art is understood as a means of interpreting experience, at the same time as it is a means of bringing new forms of experience into being. "The aesthetic 'validity' or 'unity' that we attribute to a work refers to its singularly illuminating power to open our eyes to what is seemingly familiar, to disclose anew an apparently familiar reality."[3] Art is capable of this kind of disclosure in virtue of its ability to revalue the nonethical elements of experience, making the ordinary extraordinary, the ugly beautiful, the (culturally) inconceivable conceivable. Given that genuinely ethical (generalizable) values are very few, however, the values that remain, all of which apparently belong to the aesthetic-cultural category, must be a motley collection indeed, including everything from purely sensory habits of perception to kinship values or to such cultural values as the "goals of liberal education." It is questionable that aesthetic discourse in the usual sense contains all the dimensions of a discussion of values like these, as some of them raise issues of an ethical or political nature as well. Before continuing with this particular question, it would be useful to further clarify the nature of aesthetic-expressive discourse.

Unlike truth and normative validity claims, aesthetic-expressive claims cannot be *justified* discursively or consensually (*TCA* I, 334; *CES,* 64). The vindication of an aesthetic-expressive claim holds that claim to a standard of authenticity, but a consensus on such a claim, unlike a consensus on truth or normative validity, is not a requirement for validity. In other words, the authenticity of an aesthetic-expressive validity claim does not entail that it commands universal agreement. Nonetheless, the authenticity of personal expressions is debatable, and it makes sense to speak of having genuine reasons for them.[4] For example, I may have good reasons for having and expressing a need for an education in philosophy, although it may puzzle you; I probably do not have good reasons for expressing a need for a combine harvester.

Self-expression that is both innovative and authentic, in a deeper sense than is expected in everyday interaction, becomes art, because novel interpretations of the world's meaning and value for the subject expand the range of possibilities for meaningful engagement with the lifeworld. Inauthentic expression, in contrast, is characterized by rigidity and lack of freedom. It is an expression, for Habermas, of an inability to communicate—an inability to assimilate and contribute new content to the interpretive framework provided by culture for the interpretation of experience. These are interesting suggestions, although many philosophers of art (such as the formalists) would take issue with the implication that art is a means of need interpretation or value formation; and others, seeing the potential connection between ideology, social organizations, and the available means of symbolically articulating one's needs, would prefer to look for sincerity in the expression of needs in the political rather than in the aesthetic domain.[5]

It follows from Habermas's claim of the status of a validity claim for self-expression that no one can authentically express a *purely subjective* need or response. If self-expression raises validity claims, then even personal values are defined only in discourse. This is compatible with the highly personal and private nature of some self-expression. Habermas's point seems to be, not that there is no private discourse (in the ordinary sense), but that the self-expression and interpretation involved in, for example, personal growth is inherently communicative rather than inherently subjective. Other self-expression is both personal and "public": its significance, as well as the communicative process of expression, intertwines personal with collective values. A discussion of the impact of a film or novel may be an instance. In this context, *collective* does not mean universal. Such values as the 'good life' or 'happiness' are both personal and shared collectively, though their substantive definitions are not universal, as they can be articulated only under contingent and local circumstances.

Self-expressive discourse fills an important gap left open by the definition of ethical discourse. It is obvious that not all values are generalizable, and that nongeneralizable values must be recognized, if not in a system of universal norms, then certainly in a given community's conception of the good life. It is natural to suppose that if nongeneralizable values can be judged as to their authenticity, then sincerity claims about such values (the good life, happiness) play a vital role in the definition of the totality of our collective aims as rational, social, and enculturated beings. This step, natural as it seems, leads to deep questions about the plausibility of Habermas's division of rationality into the three domains of validity. The discourse whose aim is to provide a global view of the ideal life, personal and societal, would seem to have to transcend the boundaries of those spheres of discourse attached to the particular value spheres, to include issues pertaining to our other pursuits—scientific, technical, legal and moral. The suggestion has been made that aesthetic-expressive discourse has come to play this role in Habermas's theory. David Ingram's analysis of Habermas's recent work takes the position that aesthetic rationality reconciles the distinct spheres of rational action, whose differentiation in the modern world tends to fragment our activity, rendering the critical subject capable of "holistic social critique."[6] However, because the "truth and truthfulness" of art is "mimetic" rather than discursively redeemable, "the truth of holistic social critique . . . can never be grounded discursively."[7] (The term *mimetic* is a theoretical one, whose meaning is contested, for example, in the work of Adorno and Walter Benjamin. It may be preliminarily understood here as denoting the sort of prediscursive and imitative communication that occurs in becoming conscious as a human.)

Ingram argues that Habermas's adoption of Weber's notion of three 'value spheres' leaves the three types of discourse without any means of making reference to each other. David Ingram also challenges Habermas's apparent confidence in the ability of philosophy, as reflection on reason, to "represent the lifeworld's interest in the whole complex of functions and structures connected and combined in communicative action" (*PDM,* 208).[8] A global form of rationality is necessary if we are to be able to conduct a global critique of reification or to discover the balance between functional organization and lifeworld activity that serves human interests. Neither of these enterprises is possible from within one validity domain alone. Ingram argues that to be shown "what no form of ideal speech possibly could show—namely, complete realization of a life of freedom and happiness at the level of individual and collective life," we would need to recognize instead a more global and mimetic kind of aesthetic 'truth.' Ingram finds some movement in this direction, on Habermas's part, in some of his recent writings.[9]

The significance of the role of aesthetic reason and its peculiar connection to happiness, appears most clearly in the light of

Hegel's critique of Kant's 'formalism' and 'abstract universalism.' Hegel's distinction between 'morality' (*Moralität* or moral law) and 'ethical life' (*Sittlichkeit* or the good, the happy, and the virtuous life) made evident a serious potential shortcoming in Kantian ethics. Although the categorical imperative promised a formal key to the whole of the moral law, it was bought at the price of severing all connection to the concept of happiness or the good life. (For Kant, performing an action from duty requires that the reasons for which an action is performed are indifferent to personal interests.) Thus two fundamental moral concepts were sundered: that of duty or obligation and that of happiness. This division haunts Habermas's 'discourse ethics' as well, as it mirrors a good portion of Kant's system.[10] Recently, Habermas has turned to aesthetic reason as a source of possible 'utopian discourse.' If it is to be such a discourse, however, it would need to be capable of informing the culture of the good society as a totality and not merely serve as a mode of subjective expression.

Adopting an argument of Albrecht Wellmer's, Habermas acknowledges that aesthetic experience seems to contain a "potential for truth" that does not raise any single validity claim and whose significance is not limited to any one domain of cultural life. Rather, it reveals possibilities that would transform culture and life as a whole: "[The aesthetic] validity claim admittedly stands for a *potential* for 'truth' that can be released only in the whole complexity of life-experience; therefore, this 'truth potential' may not be connected to (or even identified with) just one of the three validity claims constitutive for communicative action, as I have previously been inclined to maintain."[11] On the other hand, there are problems that accompany interpreting such remarks too strongly, imputing to aesthetic-expressive validity claims *as such* the global function found by Ingram. Habermas echoes Marcuse's and Schiller's self-warnings against investing too much in essentially aesthetic visions in the *Discourse of Modernity:* "The late Marcuse repeats Schiller's warning against an unmediated aestheticization of life: Aesthetic appearance develops reconciling force only as appearance—'only so long as he conscientiously abstains, in theory, from affirming the existence of it, and renounces all attempts, in practice, to bestow existence by means of it'" (*PDM,* 50). However art might reveal the world afresh, it seems likely that Habermas would still wish to reflect on these visions with respect to the other validity claims before admitting to any real transformative power in them. Although Ingram, Wellmer, and Habermas agree that art is capable of stimulating a kind of global reflection that raises all three validity claims at once, it is less plausible to suppose that aesthetic standards alone have the capacity to decide the validity of those revelations as aims of society, much less to overcome the need for putting alternative conceptions of society to the tests of truth and normative validity.

Communicative Action and Communicative Rationality

The three validity claims and the norms of their use together constitute the *validity basis of speech:* the basis of all rational discourse. Competence in making and vindicating validity claims is the same thing as what Habermas calls *communicative rationality.* The rest of this chapter examines this concept.

Habermas calls action oriented to mutual understanding *communicative action.* He believes that any sound sociological model of the social world and its evolution must come to terms with the importance of action oriented to mutual understanding for the construction of the shared representations, norms, and expectations that hold societies together.

Successful understanding-oriented actions are *communicatively rational.* The norms of communicative rationality include the norms of theoretical, practical, and aesthetic-practical rationality. Like any theory of rationality, such as a theory of rational choice, the theory of communicative rationality is a *normative* theory. It comprises norms that distinguish rationally defensible from rationally indefensible claims. This means that the theory can be used to determine the rationality of our commitments to particular beliefs and ethical or cultural norms. However, this also means that the theory does not necessarily describe our actual speech behavior, which may or may not be communicatively rational at any given moment. Nonetheless, as we shall see later on in this chapter, Habermas argues that all communication is, as such, inherently oriented to mutual understanding. Although this hypothesis does not entail that our actual speech behavior is always in accord with the norms of communicative rationality, it does entail that what makes communication possible—our *ability* to communicate—does rest on those norms. Habermas calls his theory of communicative competence ***universal*** or ***formal pragmatics.***[12]

Habermas believes that the norms of communicative rationality, or the "validity basis of speech," constitute the core of communicative competence. These norms are the procedural guidelines for the achievement of rational consensus (or, if not consensus, a rationally motivated mutual understanding) on truth, normative, and expressive validity claims.[13] If Habermas is right, any speaker expresses a commitment to these procedures ***and their consensual outcomes*** simply by performing speech acts. Habermas strongly believes that human social relationships are possible in virtue of implicit mutual commitments to future consensus. This hypothesis is of central importance for Habermas, because it is necessary if he is to explain the evolution of modern culture as, in part, a progressive institutionalization of these consensus-oriented norms. If he is correct, then the key to our understanding the evolution of culture is an understanding of the genesis and structure of understanding-oriented action.

To evaluate Habermas's hypothesis, we will need to answer a question that was left open in the previous chapter: Do we all share an overriding interest in achieving mutual understanding *in virtue of being capable of communication?* Before we look more closely at the act of communication, however, it would be helpful to look at a general overview of formal pragmatics.

Formal Pragmatics: An Overview

Habermas's formal pragmatics takes an unprecedented approach to the field of pragmatics. Pragmatics is the study of how language is used to communicate, as opposed to the study of language itself (as in phonology, syntax, and semantics). Research in pragmatics normally is conducted on features of the usage of a given language in a given community. Habermas's formal pragmatics is far broader: Habermas claims that the speaker's ability to communicate is derived from a pretheoretical knowledge that is universal to all speakers. Habermas calls this knowledge *communicative competence.* The task of formal pragmatics is to give a reconstruction of communicative competence.

The epistemic status of this pretheoretical knowledge is held to be similar to that of the universal linguistic competence hypothesized in Noam Chomsky's earlier work.[14] However, Habermas does claim that communicative competence is innate, or that his reconstruction of communicative competence is psychologically real. He prefers to characterize it using Gilbert Ryle's 'know-how/know-that' distinction, as an implicit know-how acquired by every competent speaker.[15]

Like linguistic competence, communicative competence must be studied by observing speech behavior, though it is never displayed, in its pure form, in actual performance. Therefore, a model of communicative competence can be obtained only by means of a process of reconstruction—by explication of the conditions necessary for the communicative achievements of speakers. A reconstruction of communicative competence may be held as adequate if it (1) is capable of accounting for all observed patterns in the (proper) usage of sentences in speech acts and (2) does not generate entailments that disagree with speakers' intuitions.[16]

Normally, pragmatics studies features of language use that are closely tied to specific local social and cultural practices. Habermas does not deny that pragmatics is the study of the social and cultural usage of language. He believes, however, that in addition to local features of usage, there are universal and formally reconstructible features of use. The most fundamental achievement of any speech act whatsoever, according to Habermas, is the offer and establishment of interpersonal (speaker-hearer) relationships. Habermas takes the ability to form speaker-hearer relationships as basic to our ability to enter into and maintain interpersonal relationships in general, whether cooperative or uncooperative, intimate or impersonal. In Habermas's view, this *generative* capacity of speakers to create and enter into speaker-hearer relationships is overlooked in theories that place pragmatics derivatively with respect to the production of indicative sentences, portraying the various ways of using language in speech acts as modifications on the representational use (*CES,* 35). Without assuming such a capacity, Habermas maintains, it is impossible to explain how speakers are able to enter into human relationships at all. In other words, the status that Habermas claims for the theory of formal pragmatics, as universal and fundamental to the use of language, amounts to the claim that there exists a universal basis for all social relationships. Thus Habermas's formal pragmatics, and his theory of society generally, presupposes that any given social relationship is possible only in virtue of the norms of communicative competence (*CES,* 35).

There are some similarities between the rules that Habermas believes underlie communication and the 'maxims of conversation' formulated by Paul Grice, a philosopher of language. Grice suggests that the maxims specify what participants have to do to converse in a maximally efficient, rational and cooperative way; namely, speak sincerely, relevantly, and clearly, providing sufficient information.[17] Habermas's description of what a speaker, in general, must know to be able to perform speech acts is stronger than Grice's maxims, as it attempts to define the conditions of possible communication, rather than the conditions of maximally efficient communication. An acceptable speech act, for Habermas, is one that raises four defensible validity claims: truth claims, normative validity claims, truthfulness or sincerity claims, and intelligibility claims (this fourth validity claim is not philosophically interesting and so is usually ignored in discussions of Habermas's theory). Because Grice's maxims do not specify that a speech act raise defensible normative validity claims (although they include truth, truthfulness, and intelligibility), Habermas would find them insufficient as a specification of the basic and universal rule knowledge of communicatively competent speakers.

Habermas's first sketch of his theory of universal pragmatics, which appeared as "Towards a Theory of Communicative Competence" in 1970, was written in response to the general semantics proposed and partially elaborated in Noam Chomsky's *Aspects of the Theory of Syntax* (1965). In this paper, Habermas argued that there are no innate semantic universals, by alluding to some work in ethnolinguistics that shows historical and cultural variances in the basic 'meaning components' of a language. However, he added, there are *dialogical* semantic universals—the *dialogue constitutive* universals—that "establish the conditions of potential communication." These universals are types of expressions that would be necessary for a language to enable the speaker to make descriptive, prescriptive, or expressive statements, such as personal pronouns, indexical terms to indicate place in time and space, performative verbs (e.g., thank) and intentional verbs (e.g., hope). At one time, Habermas suggested that a general semantics, if anything, is derivative of a theory of communicative competence: "If it were possible... to distinguish also the categorial frameworks of potential views of life in terms of distributions of dialogue-constitutive universals, then general semantics could be developed on the basis of a theory of communicative competence."[18] However, Habermas has not taken this suggestion any further in his later work.

Habermas divides the ways that sentences can be used, or the pragmatic functions of sentences, into three fundamental (and universal) categories: the use of sentences to establish speaker-hearer relationships, to represent states of affairs, and to express oneself. These functions correspond to three kinds of validity claims raised when sentences are used in any of these ways.

The ways in which sentences are used are always constrained by contextual features. Habermas holds that three of these contextual features are universal to all speech situations (that is, in all languages and cultures)—the social speaker-hearer relationship (or "I-You" relationship), a third-person relationship between the speaker and the world ("I-It"), and a reflexive relationship between the speaker and his or her own subjective world of intentions, desires, beliefs, and the like.[19] Habermas often speaks of three worlds (social, objective, subjective) toward which we can take performative, objectivating, or expressive attitudes, establishing a certain kind of relation between ourselves and each of these worlds.[20]

An example illustrating these relations might be helpful. Suppose I were to say, "Please pick up some marmalade at the market." In making this utterance, I am establishing a speaker-hearer relationship with You, whom I am asking to do me a favor; I am presupposing a self-world relationship by presupposing that some state of affairs obtains in the world (there being marmalade at the market); and I am presupposing a reflexive relation to myself, as the person who is responsible for having made a sincere request.

Each of these three aspects of speech acts are both governed and "made possible" by a particular standard of validity. Thus indicative statements are judged as true or false, performative utterances (such as commands) are judged by their conformity to the social and ethical norms governing the speaker-hearer relationships, and expressive utterances are judged as honest or sincere and dishonest or insincere. The act of making a statement, performative utterance, or expressive utterance could not be performed without at least an implicit commitment to the corresponding validity standard. Thus knowledge of how to raise and provide grounds for validity claims is the core of communicative competence.

Habermas believes that the possibility of successful communication cannot be explained unless we posit a commitment, on the part of all speakers, to such a 'validity basis of speech.' Because communication, ultimately, is the means of establishing human relationships, the validity basis of speech is also the basis of interpersonal relationships. What, specifically, provides the content of an offer of interpersonal relationships is the cognitive testability of the validity claims raised in speech acts. A successfully established speaker-hearer relationship is one that is premised on a mutual commitment to the validity basis of speech. "With their [speech] acts, speaker and hearer raise validity claims and demand that they be recognized. But this recognition need not follow irrationally, since the validity claims have a cognitive character and can be checked. I would like, therefore, to defend the following thesis: ***In the final analysis, the speaker can . . . influence the hearer and vice versa, because speech-act typical commitments are connected with cognitively testable validity claims***—that is, because the reciprocal bonds have a rational basis" (CES, 63).

The power of speech acts to influence the hearer, to offer an interpersonal relation for the hearer's acceptance, is to be explained by the existence of a rational basis or validity basis for speech. That is, if the hearer doubts the acceptability of a speech act on some ground (intelligibility, sincerity, truth, or normative correctness) there is a means for rationally resolving the doubt. Doubts concerning the truth or normative validity of an utterance can be resolved in theoretical and practical discourse, and doubts concerning its sincerity can be resolved through further observation of the speaker. It is possible for speech acts to be acceptable or unacceptable because it is possible for the hearer to affirm or reject the validity claims raised in the performance of an illocutionary act, *on rational grounds*.

Let us look at an example. Suppose A asks B to open the door. A's speech act belongs to the class of regulative speech acts. The validity claims raised directly by regulative speech acts are normative validity claims. The normative claim raised in "I request that you open the door" is a social norm. It reads, roughly: "It is socially acceptable to make requests under conditions *x,y,* and so forth." If A is thought to be a subordinate of B's, social norms very likely would render A's request unacceptable. If A considers the existence of such a social norm ethically unacceptable, then he may attempt to engage B in practical discourse on the justifiability of the norm. In any event, both speaker and hearer, according to Habermas, must share a norm they both regard as justifiable, if the speech act is to be acceptable.

In summary, universal or formal pragmatics is divided into three domains, each giving a reconstruction of the knowledge required for using sentences to perform one of the three pragmatic functions of speech. Habermas believes that, in each case, this knowledge can be characterized as the mastery of pragmatic universals (the 'dialogue-constitutive universals'). The dialogue-constitutive universals are what a speaker must know in order to be able to "embed" sentences in 'relations to reality' (to be able to say something *about* something *to* someone, *expressing* something about the speaker [CES, 29]). These abilities cannot be accounted for in a theory of *linguistic* competence, a theory that provides only what a person must know to produce meaningful and grammatical sentences. The ability to use language to communicate can be accounted for only in a pragmatic theory: "It is otherwise with [the speaker's] ability to communicate; this is susceptible only to pragmatic analysis. By 'communicative competence' I understand the ability of a speaker oriented to mutual understanding to embed a well-formed sentence in relations to reality" (CES, 29).

Does Communicative Competence Entail an Interest in Reaching Understanding?

Habermas conceives of communicative competence as the capacity to make oneself understood and to understand others and, in the ideal case, to reach an understanding in the full sense—mutual understanding or even consensus (see note 13). Habermas's conception of communicative competence also includes a belief that speech acts, in their 'original' or 'primary' form, are performed with *communicative intent* and that communicative intent is aimed at reaching understanding and, ultimately, at bringing about consensus (*TCA* I, 287–288). By engaging in communication, every speaker at least implicitly commits himself or herself to the conditions that hold for the ideal speech situation, or the validity basis of speech. The ideal speech situation offers the possibility of a rational consensual basis for interaction free of force, open or latent. Just how strong a thesis Habermas is making is visible when we recognize that it entails that a commitment to the ideal speech situation is also a commitment to a society free of coercion in any form.

The claim that communicatively competent individuals are committed to reaching understanding and ultimately to consensus denies a widespread assumption in social philosophy, namely, the assumption that any rational action can be explained as a basically self-interested individual's choice of means to some personal end. The theory of communicative competence holds that there is at least one end (mutuality) to which we are committed in virtue of being capable of communication and that this end is prior to personal ends.

Habermas has provided two kinds of support for this contention, the first deriving from a nonhistorical analysis of the structure of speech acts, and the second kind from an expansion of George Herbert Mead's historical reconstruction of the evolution of communication (TCA II, 3–42). Mead's theory analyzes the gradual emergence of symbolically mediated communication out of the 'conversation of gestures' of our prehominid ancestors and relatives, reconstructing the stunning moment, a "moment" that must have spanned centuries, in which our ancestors became aware of "meaning the same thing" as another. Because Habermas employs and extends Mead's reconstruction principally to transpose the theory of communicative competence into an historical hypothesis, I will devote most of my attention here to the first argument. However, it would be inappropriate not to include at least a brief sketch of his discussion of Mead, if only to illustrate Habermas's understanding of communicative competence as a product of historical development.

Mead traced the phylogenetic origin of symbolic communication back to the behavioral responses of vertebrate animals to the behavior of other animals. In this 'conversation of gestures,' the overt behavioral response of the second animal to the behavior of the first is the interpretation, or 'natural meaning,' of the first animal's behavior. As greater intelligence emerges, the responsive gesture comes to implicitly arouse the same response in the gesturer as it arouses in the other. The natural meaning of the gesture for the other, then, is internalized by the gesturer itself, and the gesturer acquires a primitive "awareness" of being a sender of meaningful signals. In "calling out the response in himself [that] he calls out in another," the gesturer is "taking the attitude of the other." Habermas argues that the recognition of identity between meanings cannot occur, however, until "ego knows how alter *should* respond to a significant gesture," for "it is not sufficient to expect that alter *will* respond in a certain way" (*TCA* I, 14). Without conventions for the use of symbols, ego's expectations are merely predictive.

In Mead's work, the emergence of normatively regulated behavior occurs with the ability to adopt social roles (or interchangeable patterns of meaningful behavior). For example, only if the role occupied by the sender of an imperative is conceivably interchangeable with the role occupied by the receiver can the issuing of imperatives be understood as a practice governed by norms, rather than an arbitrary imposition of the wills of particular others. Habermas incorporates this insightful hypothesis but emphasizes that the emergence of modes of usage other than those that mediate social interaction (such as assertion or self-expression) remains to be explained, and that communicative intent in its fullest sense, or the commitment to the full validity basis of speech, explains them. Raw signals are undifferentiated with respect to what is being *done* with them—whether they are imperatives, expressions of emotion, or attempts at conveying information. To differentiate among these modes of use, senders must be capable of receiving responses that are not simply arbitrary reactions to their wills—responses, in other words, that accept or challenge implied validity claims. In summary, then, Habermas uses Mead's work to illustrate, in what he hopes to be a respectable evolutionary hypothesis, that the universality of communicative intent can be seen in a historically evolving commitment to the validity basis of speech.

The first, and speech-act theoretical, argument for this commitment follows a surprising and intriguing course: Habermas claims that the communicatively competent individual's commitment to the conditions of the ideal speech situation is inherent in the *structure* of speech acts.[21] Because no speech act can be performed that does not make or presuppose such a commitment, its ends are prior to particular personal ends that are sought only contingently in the performance of a speech act. These ends—mutual understanding, knowledge of what is true and right, sincere expression, and societal legitimacy—are necessary because being communicatively competent just is having such ends, even if only imperfectly conceived. To understand this argument, it will be necessary to explain the structure and content of speech acts.

Whenever a sentence is used in an utterance by a speaker, more information is conveyed to the hearer by the utterance than is contained in the propositional content or literal meaning of the sentence uttered. Understanding the propositional content of a third person indicative sentence, for Habermas, is grasping a representation of a state of affairs. But information is also conveyed about *how* the propositional content is being used in an act; for example, to raise a question or to make an assertion. This information is necessary if the hearer is to understand what the speaker is doing by making the utterance, as well as how the hearer himself or herself ought to respond to the utterance. Some of this information conveys to the hearer that what has occurred is an act of communication. This occurs primarily by means of the use of the first and second person pronouns. Habermas assumes that the use of first and second person pronouns is at least implicit in every speech act and visible when speech acts are made fully explicit. Although, for example, we rarely preface assertions with the phrase *I assert to you that* or *I tell you that,* the content of the phrase is contained implicitly in the meaning of any assertion.

Some of the information about how a sentence is being used specifies what type of act has been performed, for example, whether the utterance raised a question, made a request, or made a statement. Speech-act types are distinguished by the type of speaker-hearer relationship being offered, or, more precisely, what kinds of responsibilities are being taken by the speaker and offered to the hearer. Habermas believes that the most fundamental of these responsibilities are the raising of validity claims by speakers and their acceptance or nonacceptance by hearers. For this reason, he classifies speech acts by the kinds of validity claims raised in performing them (*TCA* I, 319). Understanding the information that specifies the speech act type thus involves grasping the 'acceptability conditions' of a speech act, or what must be the case if the speaker's offer of a speaker-hearer relationship, with its attendent responsibilities, is acceptable.

Speech-act types are roughly indicated in speech acts by performative verbs. Performative verbs only roughly indicate speech act types, because they can be used in nonliteral ways. For example, though the verb *tell* belongs to the class of constative verbs, it can be used as a communicative, to indicate emphasis ("I tell you, he's coming now!"), as well as sarcastically, rhetorically, and so on. In such cases it is also necessary to know something about the context to know what type a speech act falls under.

Finally, there is information that conveys a specific speaker's meaning, which can be conveyed only if speaker and hearer share certain background beliefs and assumptions about a particular context. Understanding a speaker also requires familiarity with a particular context of which the utterance in question is a constitutive part: preceding, concomitant, and expected subsequent activity, the age, race, or gender of the speaker, or a social or cultural milieu, for example. Not necessarily part of the information conveyed by a speech act, but possibly required for full understanding of a speech act are the speaker's *perlocutionary aims* or intended responses by the hearer. By making a statement, A may intend to embarrass B, though A does not *signal* her intention in any conventional way.

Thus, five kinds of information are conveyed in the performance of a speech act, all of which a hearer must grasp to understand the speech act completely:

1. The information that indicates that an event is a communicative act,
2. The propositional content,

3. The indication of a speech-act type (or illocutionary act),
4. Idiosyncratic allusions to a context, and
5. Perlocutionary aims (what effect or response the speaker intends the hearer to have or make to the speech act).

A central thesis in Habermas's argument holds that perlocutionary aims are not part of utterance *meanings*. Habermas argues that understanding a speech act as though it were performed sincerely is logically prior to understanding the act as a means to some end other than communication (*TCA* I, 289ff.).

Habermas believes that the logical priority of communicative ends over noncommunicative, manipulative ends has already been established in the distinction, drawn by the well-known Oxford philosopher of language, John Austin, between illocutionary and perlocutionary acts.[22] "This will turn out to be the case only if it can be shown that the use of language with an orientation to reaching an understanding is the *original mode* of language use, upon which indirect understanding, giving someone to undertand something or letting something be understood, and the instrumental use of language in general, are parasitic. In my view, Austin's distinction between illocutions and perlocutions accomplishes just that" (*TCA* I, 288).

Perlocutionary acts are acts by means of which the speaker produces an effect upon the hearer that is related only contingently to the meaning of the utterance. For example, pointing out a mutual acquaintance across the room may have the accidental effect of reminding you of an embarrassing encounter in the past. However, this effect is hardly part of the meaning of what I said ("Look, there's Pierre"), though it may have been my *intention* to embarass you. Illocutionary acts obviously produce effects on the hearer as well, but these effects are related by convention to the type of illocutionary act performed. As they are understood by Austin, the effects produced by illocutionary acts are of three kinds: "So here are three ways, securing uptake, taking effect, and inviting a response, in which illocutionary acts are bound up with effects; and these are all distinct from the producing of effects which is characteristic of the perlocutionary act."[23] Where having these three effects is definitive of the successful speech act, perlocutionary effects occur independently of the success of the illocutionary act. In other words, it is not possible to perform an illocutionary act the success of which depends on (or whose uptake consists in) a perlocutionary effect. For example, we do not say: "I hereby humiliate you by...," *thereby* humiliating you.

For Habermas, this line of argument shows that a speaker's attempts to use language to achieve ends other than mutual understanding are derivative of actions oriented toward consensus. Habermas thinks that the success of the speech act rests on the type of communicative relationship established between the speaker and the hearer, and that this relationship is secured by the illocutionary component of the speech act. Recall that, for Habermas, an essential feature of speech acts is their ability to "influence the hearer in such a way" that the hearer "can take up an interpersonal relation" to the speaker (*CES,* 36–37). The type of interpersonal relation taken up is determined by the type of speech act performed, or, in other words, by its illocutionary component. Perlocutionary effects can occur only after the communicative relationship has been established, as though the speaker's offer of this relationship had been sincere. Thus, Habermas argues, perlocutionary aims can be satisfied only if the hearer first understands the 'manifest meaning' of an utterance, its propositional content and its illocutionary force, as if the speaker *had no* perlocutionary aims (*TCA* I, 289). Hence, communication noncontingently involves having a communicative intent, which is prior to any contingent aims.[24]

Communicative intent, as far as it is possible to tell from the text, is nothing less than a commitment to the rational validity basis of speech. Any speaker is committed to the rational validity basis of speech, *whether or not this is in accord with the speaker's expressed intentions.* The very presence of communication shows a common commitment to a rational basis for the pursuit of theoretical and practical inquiry, and for the establishment of social relations. However, the validity basis of speech itself is not the end sought by communicative intent. That end is autonomous mutuality, a form of social interaction free of arbitrary coercion and the use of deception, based on the autonomous rational motivation of each participant.

It is important to note that this claim—that communicative intent is inherent to speech acts—allows Habermas to pass from the level of the psychological explanation of communicative actions to the level of the sociological explanation of culturally held communicative practices, one of the two lines of societal evolution hypothesized in his theory of society. The communicative practices that define a culture, and the individual's communicative practices, evolve toward the very same *telos.* Communicative intent comes to shape not only the speech practices of the individual, but also, through these developments (especially when social, economic, or natural crises lends them urgency), those of the culture. As patterns of communicative interaction are constrained to some extent by the level of advancement of the material means of production, however, their development is not autonomous, but constitutes one of two interdependent processes in societal evolution.

The individual's ability to recognize, raise and defend validity claims is not entirely dependent upon the level to which the communicative practices of the culture have evolved, of course—it is true, for example, that individuals may display an 'objectivating attitude' (an orientation toward an objective world, beliefs about which raise *truth* claims) in a culture in whose communicative practices truth and normative validity claims are still relatively undifferentiated. However, as long as the objectivating attitude is not a part of the communicative ability acquired by the individual, its appearances are likely to be limited and tied to peripheral activities (*TCA* I, 44–45).

Communicative Rationality Again

The *Theory of Communicative Action* opens with a preliminary outline of the concept of communicative rationality, the key concept in Habermas's critical theory of society. The concept figures not only at the level of empirical inquiry, where Habermas pursues the question of the extent to which communicative rationality has evolved within a given society, but also at the metatheoretical and methodological levels, where it figures in the choice of the theoretical taxonomy and the framing of inquiry, as well as normatively in the inquirer's own dialogue with the subjects. The roles played by the concept of communicative rationality in Habermas's theory of societal rationalization will become clearer in the following chapter. For the moment, we shall focus upon the concept itself and what distinguishes it from the prevailing understanding of rationality.

In everyday usage, many different kinds of things are called *rational*—the term can modify actions, persons, practices, organizations, and even, at times, desires, emotional responses, and ethical principles. In general, and in many philosophical and social scientific circles, however, there is a tendency to equate rationality as a whole with the capacity to choose the optimal means to some given end. Thus a person is a rational consumer who makes purchases in such a way as to meet as many needs and preferences as possible ; an organization is rational that is arranged in such a way that the actions of its members produce the optimum attainable outcome. For Marx and Weber, societies undergo an historical process of rationalization, where rationalization is seen as an increasing ability of a society to manipulate natural and social forces in the service of class or collective ends.

Habermas calls this type of rationality *purposive* or instrumental rationality (*zweckrationalität*) and he is most emphatic in urging that this type of rationality not only *not* be seen as all there is to rationality, but also that it not be taken as the paradigm case of rationality. Communicative rationality, as opposed to this noncommunicative, goal-directed rationality, includes the abilities attached to the use of the validity basis of communication. These are not the (non-communicatively oriented) abilities to make successful instrumental choices, but the ability to make defensible judgments about the world (on which basis optimal instrumental choices are made), to establish and enter into social relationships in accord with acceptable norms, and to creatively and authentically interpret and express personal needs and interests. Successful communicatively rational actions are successful because they bring about a form of social integration—rationally based mutuality—that is essential to objective inquiry, social relationships and self-realization. "This concept of *communicative rationality* carries with it connotations based ultimately on the central experience of the unconstrained, unifying, consensus-bringing force of argumentative speech, in which different participants overcome their merely subjective views and, owing to the mutuality of rationally motivated conviction, assure themselves of both the unity of the objective world and the intersubjectivity of their lifeworld" (*TCA* I, 10). Communicative rationality, then, governs the interactions of those communities—scientific, moral, legal, and aesthetic—that negotiate the boundaries of a consensually understood world that is taken for granted by purposive rationality and nonconsensus-oriented action. Following the Kantian partition of reason, Habermas's conception of communicative rationality encompasses theoretical rationality, practical rationality, and the rationality of "authentic" self-expression. Accordingly, communicatively rational action is action oriented to understanding in one of the three domains that correspond to the validity claims: the scientific, the moral, and the aesthetic.

In concluding this chapter's discussion of communicative rationality, it would be useful to consider a global objection of Albrecht Wellmer's to Habermas's intentions regarding this notion. A critique of society is expected not only to provide a diagnosis of the pathologies of society, but also an idea of what society would look like that was free of pathology. The norms of rationality that constitute communicative rationality provide the normative force for Habermas's critique of society, and thus it is to these norms that we would turn to find the societal ideal that informs Habermas's critical theory. But Wellmer argues that the norms of communicative rationality alone are insufficient as a basis for formulating ideal forms of life.[25] Wellmer articulates the shortcoming as due to the formal-procedural nature of the standards that constitute communicative competence. Formal rules and procedures neither guarantee consensus nor guarantee that the substantive results of consensus will be emancipatory. He uses the analogy of a neurotic, who we can suppose possesses the formal competences of communicative competence, without being capable of the relatively emancipated life open to the integrated personality. The nonneurotic's "application" of the formal competences is likely to be "better" than the neurotic's, "but not necessarily more rational in any formally characterizable sense" (208).

> Since the formal structures of rationality guarantee neither the correctness of decisions (as perhaps seen in the light of later experiences), nor the possibility of resolving conflicts argumentatively, nor the meaningful or even happy life of the individual, there would be necessary, but not sufficient conditions in those formal structures of rationality for what we could call a 'good life.' Instead, the rational in the sense of the good life would distinguish itself from the rational merely in the sense of a formal structure, just as we distinguish the articulate from the illiterate, the healthy from the neurotic, the blind from the sighted or the happy from the unhappy.[26]

The upshot of Wellmer's argument by analogy is that just as there is no *formal* ideal of the nonneurotic subject, there is no such ideal of "a 'perfectly' emancipated society" (208).

Wellmer's challenge can be seen as one of many challenges to the project of the Enlightenment: to achieve emancipation and thereby, the good life, by founding society on rational principles rather than tradition. Habermas's response to these challenges, which will be discussed in greater depth in Chapter 6, is to urge the significance, for the critique of society, of the distinction between communicative rationality, on the one hand, and purposive, technical, and functional rationality, on the other. The collective activity of need and interest interpretation and the formation of both generalizable and nongeneralizable values is to Habermas a crucial part of communicatively rational action, which does not characterize purposively or functionally rational action. This need-interpreting activity is crucial if human interests, both universal and particular, are not to be subordinated to such constraints as the efficiency of the economic system, the stability of particular adminstrations, and so on. As Wellmer points out, however, this activity is only a necessary and not a sufficient condition of the "perfectly" emancipated society, understood in the strongest possible sense as one in which the good life is realized. In response to Wellmer, it is not clear that Habermas's intention was ever to provide the sufficient conditions for such a society. He recognizes, for example, that the loss of tradition in modern society entails that individuals and communities must accomplish their own reconciliation of differentiated values through reflection.[27] There is a positive side to this acknowledgment of the special difficulites accompanying life in a modern society: it is one indication that Habermas is more of a pluralist about conceptions of the good life than many of his critics recognize.

In the following chapter, communicative rationality appears in the foreground once again, though not as the object of a philosophical critique and defense, but within a hypothesis about the history of modern society. Now that we have looked at the philosophical support for his theory of theoretical, practical, and aesthetic knowledge, we will look at Habermas's picture of how society has evolved as a result of historical communicatively rational action.

CHAPTER 5

The Critique of Societal Rationalization

The *Theory of Communicative Action* is a series of extended discussions of the theories of Max Weber, George Herbert Mead, Emile Durkheim, Alfred Schutz, Georg Lukacs, and Talcott Parsons.[1] The discussions are intended to reveal the limitations of each of these theories by reconstructing the course of the theorists' inquiries. Once revealed, the limitations of the theories are explained as the consequence of hypotheses whose explanatory scope is too narrow.

This kind of writing is called *immanent critique.* As a part of Hegel's legacy, for the most part, it is not a kind of writing with which the English-speaking world is familiar. American students of philosophy, for example, normally are trained to focus on the analysis of an idea rather than its genesis, on the grounds that it would be fallacious to judge the merit of an idea on the basis of the forms it had taken throughout history (thus the term *genetic fallacy*). In fact, immanent critique conducts analysis as well, but on an idea that is first understood within the historical context of its intended purpose and the attempts made to fulfill it. The purpose of immanent critique itself is the further development of an idea, taking up and using what has been shown to be the reliable core of our understanding of it, to reassess those solutions by past theorists that seem to lead us astray.

For German philosophy in the Hegelian tradition, the principal object of immanent critique has always been the concept of rationality. This is true of Habermas's critique as well. Habermas's critique founds the concept of rationality on allegedly universal norms that govern communication. Together, these norms constitute communicative competence, and they have been the subject of the previous three chapters.

The theory of communicative competence, or universal pragmatics, provides the framework for Habermas's principal sociological hypothesis, which was developed in the course of his critique of rationality. In the *Theory of Communicative Action,* Habermas developed the hypothesis that the evolution of the modern capitalist welfare state is "a process of one-sided rationalization" (*TCA* I, p.140). This hypothesis is a departure from those theories of societal rationalization, beginning with Marx and Weber and ending with Horkheimer and Adorno, that, in his view, presuppose a one-dimensional concept of rationality as purposive rationality. Therefore, they overlook the possibility that particular dimensions of rationalization, not rationalization as a whole, may be the cause of the loss of meaning, freedom and solidarity that Weber and the Frankfurt School observe in modern societies. For Habermas, the broader concept of communicative rationality provides the framework in which it is possible to observe the one-sidedness of our current level of rationalization and to determine the nature and causes of the potential crises common to modern welfare states.

The theory of communicative competence, then, is not only intended to give a full account of the validity basis of speech—what makes possible communication, and thus all forms of social relationship. It also is intended, first, to constitute part of the *explanation* of societal evolution by identifying, in communicative competence, a historical force—the impetus behind increasing cultural complexity and toward ever more liberated forms of social interaction and integration. Second, the theory of communicative competence and the concept of communicative rationality are intended to provide the basis for the *critical analysis* of the level of rationalization attained by modern society. These twin purposes of the theory of communicative competence in his theory of society are intertwined in Habermas's proposed social scientific method, producing a social theory that is consciously activist in nature. Theoretical inquiry into societal evolution, in revealing the historical forces underlying societal evolution, is also critically engaged as an active participant in societal change.

Habermas argues that any critical theory of society must employ communicative rationality at three levels. At the metatheoretical level, the categories of discourse associated with each of the validity claims figure centrally in the theoretical taxonomy and supply the framework in which distinct forms of cultural learning may be analyzed.

At the methodological level, the critical theorists must interpret the behavior of their subjects as rational actions, to gain an understanding of the content of a culture. A rational interpretation is reached by participation in a dialogue with the subjects based on mutual commitment to the norms of communicative rationality. "An interpreter cannot, therefore, interpret expressions" that raise validity claims or represent the shared knowledge of a community, "without taking a position on" those validity claims (*TCA* I, 116). This dialogue contains critical potential, because it ultimately is oriented toward achieving an intersubjectivity from which the opacities caused by distorted communication have been removed.

Finally, the critical theorist must determine the *empirical* validity of the historical-sociological hypothesis that the evolution of structures of consciousness is to be understood in terms of communicative rationality and the constraints imposed on the development of those structures by functional or systemic rationalization.

In the introduction to volume I of the *Theory of Communicative Action,* Habermas claims that any adequate theory of society must invoke communicative rationality at each of these three levels (*TCA* I, 7). Essentially, this amounts to the claim that an adequate explanation of the evolution of modern society views the development of culture as a process of rationalization. From this perspective, the crisis tendencies in modern societies will be analyzed as the outcome of systematic distortions in communicative processes, caused by a tendency in modern societies to one-sided rationalization. The purposes of this chapter shall be (1) to convey, in the remainder of the introduction, the content of this hypothesis; (2) to introduce, in the following two sections, the dual method proposed for the sociological research of this hypothesis; (3) to illustrate, at the end of the third section, how Habermas's theory of society invokes the concept of rationality in the three ways just mentioned; and (4) to explain the significance of this hypothesis as a critical analysis of modern society. Finally, in the last section, I will address (5) Habermas's defense, in the *Theory of Communicative Action,* of his approach to sociological theory construction against other approaches.

Habermas challenges the classical Marxist view that the rationalization of forms of social interaction (relations of production) occurs as a function of developments in productive technology. Unlike Marxist determinists, Habermas wishes to show that changes in the forms of social interaction, and specifically in the social norms on which their existence rests, are effected within communicative interaction. On the other hand, he wishes to acknowledge that these changes are externally constrained by the demands of functional rationality (the forces of production). Where for Marx the laws of progress in material production are the fundamental laws of history, Habermas holds that society "reproduces itself" (or provides for its own continuity and further development) in two domains, each having its own "developmental logic": the domain of material reproduction, and the domain of symbolic reproduction. Developments in material reproduction follow the "logic" of functional rationality and are achieved in modern societies by *systems*—specifically, the economic and administrative systems. The evolution and behavior of these systems can be explained functionally, as they tend to be organized to perform functions such as political and economic stability and prosperity. Symbolic reproduction, on the other hand, follows the logic of communicative rationality and is achieved by building and maintaining consensus about acceptable needs and interests, social and ethical norms, and cultural traditions within the *lifeworld.* Symbolic reproduction is a discursive process, not to be explained as the outcome of functional laws, but as an evolving interpretive framework. The domain of symbolic reproduction is the source of "meaning"—the significance and value that actions, traits, objects, and events possess for the members of a community. A functionalist explanation of the systems that integrate the complex interactions within a society is not genuinely explanatory, for Habermas, unless one first achieves an understanding of the lifeworld of that society from the participant's point of view, for the limits of the participant's point of view and the norms on which it is based are limiting conditions on the development and differentiation of the economic and administrative systems.[2] Some examples of the ways in which the extent to which the lifeworld is evolved has posed limits on the differentiation of the economic and administrative systems will appear in the following two sections.

Habermas's method, then, is a dual one: a synthesis of functionalism and the *Verstehenden* or hermeneutical tradition in the philosophy of social science. Habermas believes that such a synthesis is necessary if we are to be able to grasp the form of distorted communication characteristic of the postindustrial welfare state at the most general level—as the "colonization of the lifeworld." Harbermas argues that there is a tendency in the modern welfare state for monetary exchanges and administrative procedures to replace communicative processes, resulting in the breakdown of interpersonal relationships, but that this form of distorted communication cannot be identified and explained unless one recognizes the system and the lifeworld as having *distinct* developmental "logics," the first of which must be explained functionally and the second of which—the "logic" of communicative rationality itself—understood hermeneutically. This holds, for Habermas, because these distortions just are developments in which processes that properly belong to material reproduction begin to take over functions properly belonging to the communicative procedures in the lifeworld. The takeover of the irreplaceable communicative functions of the lifeworld by systems is what Habermas calls the "colonization of the lifeworld," a form of alienation unique to advanced postindustrial capitalism.

The Lifeworld and the Method of Understanding

The term *lifeworld* derives from phenomenology. Introduced by Husserl, who attempted to construct a transcendental deduction of the intersubjectivity of knowledge and hence of a shared 'social reality' or 'lifeworld,' the term was adopted by Alfred Schutz, who worked from the assumption that there is a shared social reality.[3] Schutz thought that Husserl's transcendental deduction, and the attempt to find the origin of the lifeworld in the subject, was misled. He avoided claiming that the intersubjectivity of knowledge could be derived from transcendental features of a single consciousness, choosing instead to take the 'natural attitude' as an unquestioned given and attempt to discern general structural features of that attitude. "The sciences that would interpret and explain action and thought must begin with a description of the foundational structures of what is prescientific, the reality which seems self-evident to men remaining within the natural attitude. This reality is the everyday life-world."[4]

Habermas believes that Schutz, by failing to give an explicit account of the "foundational structures" of the natural attitude (which, for Habermas, are captured in his notion of comunicative competence), implicitly retained the monological Husserlian conception of the genesis of the lifeworld (*TCA* II, 129ff.). Husserl, whose transcendental phenomenology adopts much of Kant's transcendental psychology, locates the foundational structures of the natural attitude in the subject's capacity for consciousness. Habermas finds the basic categories of the natural attitude in the invariable "conditions of the possibility of communication" described by the theory of communicative competence (*TCA* II, 120–126). For Habermas, then, the lifeworld is a shared social construct, constituted through communication, and the universal features of communicative acts set the parameters on the constitution of lifeworlds.

The basic categories of the natural attitude correspond to the relationships (being about something, to someone, by someone) invariably established in the performance of the component acts (propositional, illocutionary, and expressive) of speech acts by the communicatively competent individual. The ability to orient oneself to the ordered unity of the objective world, to participate in the intersubjective world, and to attain ego identity—the basic abilities that constitute communicative competence—are, for Habermas, the capacities out of which the natural attitude develops.

The development of each of these capacities is a communicative process. Membership in a lifeworld entails possession of culturally transmitted knowledge: scientific, artistic-literary, and moral-legal; and also the ability to establish and enter into social relationships, guided by accepted social and ethical norms. Finally, the means of subjective expression are socialized, as the individual internalizes an interpretive framework for the interpretation of his or her needs and interests. The communicative functions fulfilled by the lifeworld, grouped under the heading "symbolic reproduction," then, are cultural reproduction, social integration, and socialization. This characterization of the lifeworld and its functions is elaborated by drawing on the work of G. H. Mead and Emile Durkheim on ego and group identity formation, processes that receive little notice in Husserl and Schutz.

The symbolically mediated processes of the lifeworld cannot be observed directly or inferred from the observation of nonlinguistic behavior, but rather must be interpreted. Therefore, the theorist is in the position of "interpreting an interpretation," or performing a "double" hermeneutic task: of arriving at an understanding of actions that are already embedded in and intelligible only in virtue of, a particular understanding of the social world (*TCA* I, 110). The theorist who is to understand the lifeworld and the nature of the processes of meaning generation in each of its three domains (culture, society, personality), and not merely to parrot the interpretions held by the participants, must employ an interpretive method that reflects the "developmental logic" of each of these domains. If, as Habermas believes, the basic competences contained in communicative competence are the foundation of these developmental logics, it may be assumed that they would provide such a method.

The interpretation of the lifeworld is intended to identify the ways in which the functions of the lifeworld are performed, because this is indispensible in acquiring a grasp of the genuine possibilities for societal change available from the perspectives of individuals and institutions within the lifeworld. For Habermas, this question is also a question of the degree to which the lifeworld is *rationalized.*

The thesis that societies undergo a process of rationalization is a longstanding article of faith in German social theory. Habermas, however, wants to distinguish between the ways in which the lifeworld and social systems (the economy and the administration) undergo rationalization. Where systems evolve in accord with the demands of functional rationality, as we shall see later, the rationalization of the lifeworld, according to Habermas, can be understood only in terms of the inclusive notion of communicative rationality, which underlies the three functions of the lifeworld.

Although all communicative action is premised on mutual recognition of the validity basis of speech, the degree to which the three validity claims are differentiated in the communicative practices of societies varies. Lifeworlds in which the distinct types of discourse made possible by each of the validity claims (theoretical, practical and aesthetic-expressive) are well differentiated are highly rationalized; lifeworlds in which the validity claims are undifferentiated are not rationalized. (It is important to point out that the degree of rationalization of a lifeworld is not intended to entail corresponding upper limits on the cognitive development of individuals.) In a society in which the different validity claims have not been differentiated, the interpretive framework to which the individual is introduced does not distinguish, for example, between the unity of an objective world and the unity of the intersubjective social world. "From this reciprocal assimilation of nature to culture and conversely culture to nature, there results, on the one hand, a nature that is outfitted with anthropomorphic features, drawn into the communicative network of social subjects, and in this sense humanized, and on the other hand, a culture that is to a certain extent naturalized and reified and absorbed into the objective nexus of operations of anonymous powers" (*TCA* I, p. 47). The development of techniques for magical influence is a natural, even logical, choice given a world-view structured by analogies between human relationships and natural events. This discussion draws heavily on Lévi-Strauss's structuralist analysis of the mythical—and for Lévi-Strauss, largely analogical—understanding of the world.

The range of a society's capacity to adapt and change is constrained by the level to which the lifeworld has been rationalized. From the perspective of certain stages of lifeworld rationalization, certain options for the rationalization of the system are not available. For example, according to Weber, had there not developed a world-rejecting, active ascetic ethic, neither the capital base (formed by savings) nor the motivation to use savings rationally in productive investment could have arisen, and these bases of the modern capitalist economy would not have emerged.[5] As another example, a society in which social relationships are rooted primarily in the culture of loyalty to feudal authority would not be able to sustain commitment to the authority of constitutional law.

The same holds, in more specific terms, for the forms that the institutionalization of a particular relationship, such as the exchange relationship, may take. In modern societies, for example, the regulating principles of the exchange relationship and the administrative position, as a result of historical development, have become *ethically neutral.* As a result, "interactions *within* the sphere of labor of one's calling are morally neutralized to the degree that communicative action can be detached from norms and values and switched over to the success-oriented pursuit of one's own interests" (*TCA* I, p.229). This development in the history of Western society is due to the emergence of the Protestant ethic. According to Habermas (and Weber, from whom many of these observations are taken), the free market economy of modern society was not an option before the emergence of the Protestant ethic, because the lifeworld had not been sufficiently rationalized; more specifically, because technical rationality had not yet been differentiated sufficiently from conventional morality. An ethically neutral set of regulatory principles, necessary for the institutionalization of corporate and administrative relations, is possible only where the distinction between the moral and the legal has been made. This distinction was made available by the Protestant ethic, in which the individual's relationship to God and overall success in the world, but not the particular activities engaged in within the world, are of ethical significance.[6]

In modern society, functional rationality—the norms of the "rational organization"—has become relatively autonomous from the processes of the lifeworld. This development has occurred because cooperation in the pursuit of economic ends came to be grounded, with the Protestants, not in ethical requirements but in the ethically neutral terms of legally binding contracts. The evolving autonomy of functional rationality has made possible what Habermas calls the *uncoupling* of the lifeworld from the system in modern societies (*TCA* II, 153). It is characteristic of modern societies that the system, organized on the basis of relationships governed by ethically neutral regulations, has disengaged itself from the consensual basis of the lifeworld.

The uncoupling of the system from the lifeworld is possible only given that individuals are capable of adopting attitudes that disengage them from the consensually based expectations of their lifeworld communities. In particular, individuals must be capable of adopting a generalized "membership" role, or general willingness to follow directives unrelated to their own particular experiences, dispositions and goals.[7] To become a member of an organization, then, is to adopt a neutral attitude toward the cultural or traditional background in which one has been socialized and socially integrated. Habermas's argument that developments in the system are enabled by the level of rationalization of the lifeworld is exemplified here in his claim that the disengagement of the role player is possible only given the institutionalization, in the lifeworld, of the ethically neutral regulation of action.

The System and Functional Explanation

Although an interpretation of the lifeworld can be given from within the lifeworld, it is not possible to give a rational reconstruction of the process of rationalization without looking at the external constraints imposed on rationalization, which are visible only when society is understood as a *system.*

The functionalist and "systems-theoretic" aspect of Habermas's theory is taken from Talcott Parsons's general theory of action.[8] The great attraction of systems theory is its ability to model (and ideally, to explain) the behavior of and interactions between complex organizations, without relying on the assumption that all the consequences of their actions are intended by their members. In other words, systems theory takes account of the likelihood that the behavior of the economic-adminstrative system of the modern welfare state cannot be explained as one would explain the choices of a rational and informed agent. The peculiar attraction of Parsons' theory is its bold (though excrutiatingly general) attempt at an integrated model of the interaction between several distinct levels of organization, from the organization of the individual organism and personality to that of the culture and the society, through media of exchange or "steering media." For Habermas, money and power are the steering media, so-called because transactions in either medium tend to redirect activity (flooding the market, for example, reduces prices, which affects consumer behavior). Behavior in the economic and administrative systems is governed by the laws that regulate transactions in the media of money and power. Unlike Parsons, however, Habermas does not model culture and personality as systems, because in his view the development of culture and personality must be understood as a communicative process rather than a functional one. Drawing from Weber, who found the principal arena of modern societal rationalization in the economy and the state, Habermas analyses the social system into two subsystems; the economic subsystem and the administrative subsystem.

For Habermas, the concept of a system provides a framework from which broad historical patterns in societal evolution become visible, which are invisible from the perspective of the lifeworld. Systems are means of "functionally integrating" the actions of individuals, and the consequences of functionally integrated actions often extend throughout the system in ways that are counterintuitive and inaccessible from the individual's perspective.

An agent's actions can be "integrated" with the actions of others in two ways: they can be socially integrated, by bringing the agents' dispositions into concord through communication, or "functionally integrated," by regulating the agents' actions in such a way as to efficiently bring about some desired end.[9] Because the functional integration of actions can be achieved without the agents' being aware of the contribution that their activities are making to the achievement of the system goal, the functional integration of actions is more precisely described as the integration of *action consequences.*

The actions of organizations within each of the subsystems in modern society are "steered" by the institutionalized media of money and power. Economic exchange occurs within the medium of money, and administrative actions within the medium of the power attached to positions in "rational" organizations. The institutionalization of money in property and contract law and the institutionalization of powers attaching to offices make possible the establishment of relationships based not on mutual commitment to the possibility of rational consensus, but on acceptance of the terms of the contract or the duties of an office. Thus unloosed from the consensual requirements of the lifeworld, activity within the system can proceed in accord with the goal-oriented requirements of the system alone. Note again that this tendency for functional systems to "uncouple" from the lifeworld is one of the basic characteristics of all modern societies, in Habermas's view.

The economic system, based on standardized exchange relationships, and the administrative system, based on supervisory authority or power, are the outcome of an evolutionary process. As the means of material production develop, the relations of production adapt by evolving divisions of labor, and the need arises to regulate the exchange of the products of the various specialized producers. Furthermore, exchange must be administrated in a way that enhances production to the greatest possible extent, given the adaptive options available to the relations of production.

As the division of labor progresses, it becomes necessary to delegate positions that oversee the various specialized activities within an organization, providing for their efficient integration. Thus societies undergoing progressive division of labor must institutionalize both the exchange relationship and positions of organizational authority or power. "The authoritative combination of specialized performances requires delegating the authority to direct, or *power,* to persons who take on the tasks of organization; the functional exchange of products calls for the establishment of *exchange relationships.* Thus a progressive division of labor is to be expected only in action systems that make provisions for the *institutionalization of organizational power and exchange relationships*" (*TCA* II, 160). The particular forms that functionally defined relationships may take, however, are constrained by factors external to mere "functional optimality." The system and the lifeworld are linked: the existence of functionally defined relationships is premised on a highly rationalized lifeworld (Recall the dependence of the modern capitalist economy on the differentiation between morality and legality.) Specifically, the system depends on the fact that the lifeworld has prepared its members ethically, socially, motivationally, and technically for their "functional roles."

Habermas's theory of social evolution locates the forces of historical societal change in the evolving relationship between changes in the lifeworld and changes in the system—between the progressive innovations in the functional integration of actions or system differentiation (serving the development of the means of material reproduction) and the progressive rationalization of forms of social integration in the lifeworld (serving the development of the means of symbolic reproduction). Habermas believes that only by casting the rationalization of society as two distinct but interacting processes of rationalization can an explanatory theory of the evolution of modern capitalist society be attempted.

> It directs our attention to empirical connections between stages of system differentiation and forms of social integration. It is only possible to analyze these connections by distinguishing mechanisms ofcoordinating action that harmonize the *action orientations* of participants from mechanisms that stabilize non-intended interconnections of actions by way of functionally intermeshing *action consequences*.... This distinction between a *social integration* of society, which takes effect in action orientations, and a *systemic integration,* which reaches through and beyond action orientations, calls for a corresponding differentiation in the concept of society itself.... [On the one hand] society isconceived from the perspective of acting subjects as the *lifeworld of a social group*.... In contrast, from the observer's perspective of someone not involved, society can be conceived only as a *system of actions* such that each action has a functional siginificance according to its contribution to the maintenance of the system. (*TCA* II, 117)

Habermas's choice of two perspectives from which to theorize—the participant-observer's and the "uninvolved" observer's perspectives, each with its own distinct method (interpretation and functional explanation)—then, ultimately is justified on the grounds that the object domain of the theory, society itself, demands such treatment. According to Habermas, it would not be possible to understand or explain social evolution without using both perspectives and methods, because each has exclusive access to one of the two processes in societal evolution.

The claim was introduced at the beginning of this chapter that "any sociology that claims to be a theory of society has to face the problem of rationality simultaneously on the metatheoretical, the methodological, and the empirical levels." In summary, it has been illustrated that the concept of communicative rationality is employed in the hypothesis chosen at the metatheoretical level: the functional rationalization of the system presupposes the development of communicative rationality in the lifeworld—the developing ability to orient oneself to an objective world, to be mastered instrumentally, and to an intersubjective world, which provides the means for social integration (in both the lifeworld and the system) and identifies the interests to be pursued by the system. In addition, some historical evidence has been provided in support of the claim that modernization has been the outcome of a dual process of system and lifeworld rationalization. Communicative rationality enters into the social theorist's inquiry at the methodological level as well: the theorist shares the commitment to the validity basis of speech, and his or her analysis of the process of societal rationalization, therefore, is critically engaged. Due to this critical engagement on the part of the theorist, the theory of societal evolution offers not only an explanation of the emergence of the modern capitalist welfare state, but an analysis of the distortions of communication inherent to it and the potential for removing them. This feature of Habermas's theory of society shall be the focus of the following section.

The Critique of Modern Society

A critical theory of societal rationalization, as envisioned by Habermas, is intended to reveal the character and causes of the "crisis tendencies" peculiar to modern capitalist societies, as well as to indicate the potential present in modern society for further rationalization—that is, the potential for resolving these impending crises (*TCA* II, 375). Habermas understands the crisis tendencies of modern capitalist society as relative to the present stage in the uncoupling of the system and the lifeworld from each other. These tendencies are due to the assimilation, by systems of functionally integrated actions (performed within the nonlinguistic medium of the system) of tasks that inherently belong to the lifeworld—tasks that can be achieved only through communication based on a set of shared values. The assimilation of lifeworld tasks by systems results in systematic distortions of communication, as the fluid processes of cultural value formation are replaced by fixed, noncommunicative bureaucratic procedures. Habermas calls this assimilation the ***colonization of the lifeworld.***

Why then should the system colonize the lifeworld? Ironically, the tendency of systems in modern welfare states to take over lifeworld functions is a result of public demand—demand for administrative repairs to the disruptions to the lifeworld caused by fluctuations and other developments in the economy. For example, periodic recessions raise the need for a support system to respond to the resulting rise in unemployment. Price volitility in particular industries, such as housing and health care, engenders a need for regulation in the form of subsidies, price controls, or even nationalization of the industry. Also, the degree to which postindustrial societies have advanced in technology and functional differentiation entails a corresponding need for infrastructure (schools, transportation, and so forth) provided by some collective body, almost always the government. When the administration provides these services, economic crises may emerge indirectly as budgetary crises, posing the dilemma for the administration of choosing between loss of legitimacy in the eyes of the public, and even greater interference (for example, through taxes, control of capital formation, and other forms of regulation) in the private economy.

Public as well as private demands for the facilitating role of the administration in the market economy are ultimately contradictory, putting increasing pressure on the partnership between the administrative and economic systems. In addition to economic crises, Habermas identifies three other types of crisis tendencies that characterize the partnership between the postindustrial economy and the welfare state.[10] First, economic crises can be displaced into the administrative subsystem, where they emerge as "rationality crises," so named because in this domain the "deficits" are not in the first instance financial, but rational, and usually are produced by paradoxical demands on the state (*LC,* p. 62). Because the administration's claim to legitimacy in a welfare state rests on successfully shielding the majority from multiple threats of financial disaster, the failure do to so can result in loss of legitimacy, or "legitimation crisis" (*LC,* 46–47). Here, the system is caught in a vicious circle. Its strategy against the ups and downs of the economy, namely, the introduction of new regulations and programs, tends to undermine the culturally defined normative basis of the lifeworld by displacing communicative action, and as a result, the system comes to provoke the expectation that it also reestablish the social and cultural stability that it tends to undermine. (The "family agenda" of the "New Right" in the United States provides an illuminating example here.) The welfare state system threatens social structures essential to socialization into a liberal capitalist society and, therefore, is in danger of defeating itself. Because the state depends on stable socialization processes in the lifeworld, its interference in those processes is dysfunctional for the system itself. Such system dysfunctions manifest themselves within the lifeworld as perceived threats to the legitimacy of the system. In summary, society's expectations of the welfare state are destined to be unmet, as it can stabilize the economic effects of the inherently destabilizing tendencies of the free market economy only at great expense and only at the cost of destabilizing the very social and cultural values on which its existence depends.

The fourth kind of crisis concerns these values themselves. The attempts of the market-administration partnership to avoid crisis are self-undermining in that they contribute to the erosion of motives and attitudes on which the market and the administration depend. Possessive individualism, the achievement ideology and orientation to exchange value are based on traditional values such as the Puritan Ethic, expectations of justice, and universal participation in the labor market, respectively. These values are undermined by the very system that depends on them, producing "motivation crises."[11]

All four crisis tendencies are causally related, though the occurrence of one type of crisis does not necessarily entail the occurrence of any of the others. Ultimately, the causal roots are deeper: the crisis-prone partnership between the market economy and the administration of the welfare state is a class compromise that relocates and transforms the economic, depoliticized form of class conflict identified by Marx.[12] Habermas's analysis of the ultimate roots of the instability of this compromise draws on Marx's law of the falling rate of profit and its incorporation into the political economic critique of the contemporary German political economist Claus Offe.[13] Habermas, along with other observers of the modern capitalist welfare state, is uncertain about whether features of the welfare state not anticipated by Marx (for example, the contributions to the production of surplus value made by administrative support, in the form of education and research) will be capable of postponing the emergence of these crises.[14]

In summary, the colonization of the lifeworld is neither an irrational process nor the result of a "sinister dark side" of rationalization, but the natural outcome of the general functional rationality of modern societies responding to the particular way in which the class conflict has been institutionalized in the capitalist welfare state. Revealing systematic distortions of communication in the modern capitalist society is thus a matter of identifying the point at which the use of functional rationality in regulating action becomes *illegitimate* (socially or politically unacceptable) from the perspective of the lifeworld and *dysfunctional* to the system. According to Habermas, the consensus-based social organizations that constitute the lifeworld cannot be assimilated to systems of functionally integrated action without both dysfunctionalities in the system and legitimation problems from the perspective of the lifeworld. Underlying both of these problems is the erosion of culture in modern societies.

A major difficulty in assessing these hypotheses arises from the ambiguities in Habermas's writing concerning what, in the actual world, counts as a part of a system, what as part of a lifeworld, and thus what counts as an instance of the colonization of the lifeworld. For Habermas, a paradigm case is provided by the juridification (*Verrechtlichung*) of communicative processes (*TCA* II, 356–373). The juridification of communicative processes is observable as a macroscopic tendency, in modern societies, to make ever more of the decisions about lifeworld affairs as though they concerned legal technicalities only. Essentially, it is a process in which decision making is disengaged from the validity basis of speech and given a procedural, juridical basis incapable of responding to problems in any but highly standardized ways. Some specific domains of lifeworld activity that, in Habermas's view, have experienced juridification are the handling of social service cases, the handling of conflicts within families and schools, and the making of child custody decisions (*TCA* II, 367–369). Further examples of the colonization of the lifeworld might be furnished by some aspects of the medical care and old-age care industries (for example, the medicalization of the means of need interpretation in pregnancy, childcare, and elderly patient care), and the pressure on educational institutions to "uncouple" themselves "from the fundamental right to education and to close circuit [themselves] with the employment system," or, in other words, to treat schools like corporations.[15] It has been suggested that the means of need interpretation have been "medicalized" in such areas as pregnancy and childcare, and that greater life expectancy has been accompanied by increasing reliance in old age on public funds and services.[16]

Nancy Fraser discusses child rearing as an example of a task that crosses the boundary between cultural reproduction in the lifeworld and material reproduction in the system, revealing some probletic aspects of Habermas's distinction.[17] Child rearing would seem to be a lifeworld task par excellence: a primary aspect of child rearing is the successful social integration of children, and social integration depends on the acquisition of the value commitments essential to a person's ability to maintain and establish interpersonal relationships in a given community. And yet, other aspects of child rearing are closely bound to the realm of material necessity—children are also material, after all. Her examination of the lack of fit between Habermas's distinction and the case of child rearing yields some important insights—most important, that Habermas's system-lifeworld distinction mirrors the distinction, central to androcentric analyses of society, between men's paid "work," and women's unpaid "services."

The case of child rearing and day care is a good one for trying out Habermas's hypothesis. Supposing as Habermas might that the allocation of child-raising tasks to day-care facilities counts as a case of colonization of lifeworld tasks, it would follow that there is some systematic distortion of communication in this practice. A general way of stating the claim might be to say that education in the value commitments of the community cannot be achieved by functionally coordinating the unintended consequences of a child's actions with a system. But in what specific way does the institutionalization of day care distort communication?

The colonization of the lifeworld is a process in which communication is replaced by exchanges or transactions in a nonlinguistic systemic medium, such as money. This could be taken to mean that a price is put on some communicative task, and its performance is sold as a service. But if the term *replacement* is taken seriously, this cannot be what is meant. If consensus-oriented communication is *replaced with* the exchange of money (or some other transaction in a system medium), then that communication no longer takes place. The functionally integrated system (the free market economy, for example) has taken over the task, and it is no longer achieved through communication. But as Fraser points out, such a replacement does not necessarily, or even usually, occur in the case of day-care facilities.

This does not mean, however, that such replacements could not occur. It depends on what ends are being pursued, and how those ends were determined. Suppose that day-care facilities are so constrained by the requirements of survival in the free market that education, and the provision of an environment in which children could learn their way about in the world in consonance with their own emerging abilities, is a lesser priority of the facility. In such a case, we could say that the system, by denying the priority of the provision of these services, has substituted system goals for lifeworld ones.

It may be more to the point, then, to characterize the colonization, or the improper assimilation of lifeworld tasks, by the system of the lifeworld as cases in which system goals *take priority* over lifeworld ones, where the fulfillment of those lifeworld goals is essential to the maintenance of the lifeworld and, by way of the dependence of the system on the stable functioning of the lifeworld, to the maintenance of the system itself. One requirement on a day-care facility, then, would be that those who managed it be well versed in and committed to the communicative and normatively grounded ways of the lifeworld. In short, an increasing reliance on day-care facilities in the upbringing of children would be legitimate as long as these facilities not only did not interfere with the communicative process of need interpretation and the securing of the normative basis for social integration, but also recognized the priority of these processes in child care. Were day-care facilities not to fulfill these conditions, reliance on them could undermine the normative basis of the society, without providing any alternative normative basis (or the means of achieving one) to take its place.

Habermas acknowledges that there may exist organizations that (at least temporarily) do fulfill these conditions, but claims that there is a tendency among them toward ever greater integration into the system, and consequently, a tendency to abandon obligations to the lifeworld and to the primacy of the achievement of consensus over system efficiency (witness the experience of many cooperative food stores begun in the 1970s). Only where systematization is complemented by adaptive change or rationalization of the lifeworld (and, by implication, where it *allows* for and does not block such adaptation) does it avoid generating communication distortions.

The system assimilation of socially integrative processes suppresses the expression of generalizable interests, by hindering and distorting communication and by subordinating consensus oriented (communicative) action to system goals. Because social relationships are held together by norms, generalizable interests need to be brought to light to discover and vindicate the basic ethical principles of society. Furthermore, they need to be brought to light in order to clarify the social limits on systematization—to guide the formation of institutions and to provide a social basis for the functioning of those institutions. When the communicative processes by which these interests are discovered are replaced by systemic media, *reification,* a form of alienation, occurs.

Reification or objectification as it is traditionally conceived is an epistemological concept—it denotes an epistemological error. Marx, for example, claimed that capital is reified labor, and the true nature of capital is masked by ideology.[18] Habermas wishes to depart from the analysis of reification as a form of consciousness, to be overcome by a theory that translates "from one language into the other" (*TCA* II, 374). In his view, it is not labor, but consensually based social relationships that are reified when they are replaced by the standardized relationships conducted within the noncommunicative media of the system. There is an "error" here as well, but not an epistemological one. The error is made when the validity basis adduced in the lifeworld for cultural values, social relationships, and individual self-expression are replaced by the requirements of functional rationality. As long as functional rationality regulates the pursuit of the ends of material reproduction, its use is functional, but when it replaces consensus-oriented processes with efficiency-oriented processes, it reifies or rigidifies the very source of social integration on which it depends.

The positive side of Habermas's critique of reification is an argument in favor of freeing communicative action so that knowledge of the lifeworld may be used to socially control the priorities set for the operation of the system. A society that allows its ends to be determined by the survival requirements of the system and uses "technical" knowledge of social behavior ("human resources" theory, behavior management theory) to achieve them is a society that commits the error of reification. Systematization, according to Habermas, ultimately must be socially controlled, and its ends determined not by the survival requirements of the system, but by rational consensus.

This analysis of the content and cause of alienation diverges interestingly from both Weber's and Marx's analyses. For Weber, alienation is the loss of meaningfulness as social and economic institutions become increasingly rational, designed to meet secular ends. Weber's 'thesis of disenchantment' or 'loss of meaning' was influential in the shaping of the Frankfurt School's critical theory of modern society.[19] Weber, like some members of the Frankfurt School, understood meaning as ultimately religious or sacred in nature. In Habermas's view, however, the valuative basis of culture, which gives social positions, practices, and events their significance and meaning, need not be sacred. Alienation occurs when the dominant influences in societal rationalization are those of functional rationalization (rationalization of the means of material reproduction), while this form of rationalization not only remains impervious to, but also impedes, the communicative processes essential to the formation and establishment of culturally shared values. The Frankfurt School and Weber were unable to consider this possibility because "they remained fixated on the model of purposive rationality and, for that reason, did not expand the critique of instrumental reason into a critique of functionalist reason."[20] This criticism by Habermas of Weber and the Frankfurt School will be explained in the following section.

Marx's analysis of alienation is correct, in Habermas's view, insofar as it identifies the cause of alienation in the subordination of the individual to noncommunicatively determined pursuits. However, Habermas believes that the character of this subordination is incompletely analyzed in Marx, due to two assumptions that overextend the theoretical role of purposive-instrumental rationality. First, Habermas argues, Marx assumes a unity between the system and the lifeworld that results in a failure to distinguish between reification and the structural differentiation of the lifeworld, which must characterize any modern society.[21] Second, Marx assumes that goal-directed rationality, embodied in the forces of production, explains the development of forms of social integration, or relations of production. For Habermas, on the other hand, forms of social integration are established communicatively, on the basis of mutual normative and valuative commitments, and communication is a source of new productive relations.

> Whereas Marx localized the learning processes important for evolution in the dimension of objectivating thought—of technical and organizational knowledge, of instrumental and strategic action, in short, of *productive forces*—there are good reasons meanwhile for assuming that learning processes also take place in the dimension of moral insight, practical knowledge, communicative action, and the consensual regulation of action conflicts—learning processes that are deposited in more mature forms of social integration, in new *productive relations,* and that in turn first make possible the introduction of new productive forces. (*CES,* 97–98)

The powerlessness of the laborer, then, is not merely the loss of and subsequent subordination to the product of his or her labor, it is the failure of participation in the communicative processes of need interpretation and unconstrained social integration that could provide the basis for bringing the pursuit of technological advances to the fulfillment of collective ends. In the modern capitalist welfare state, government intervention, by averting the crises inherent in unbridled free market capitalism, has masked this distortion of communication, but only at the price of engendering another: the welfare state has created a subculture of dependency that remains communicatively disenfranchised.

Although need interpretation, as one of the communicative processes of the lifeworld, is hampered or distorted in the colonization of the lifeworld by the system, Habermas believes that the ideological (primarily mythical and religious) barriers to legitimate need interpretation that occur in premodern societies generally have lost their hold on modern societies. Distortions of communication in modern society are systemic, rather than ideological. This contention and Habermas's framework for the analysis of the pathologies of modern society, have been challenged from several, some highly original, perspectives. James Bohman argues that ideological distortions persist and attempts to recover from the universal pragmatics some guidelines for the critique of ideology.[22] Daniel Hallin reflects on the difficulties of putting undistorted communication into practice in the age of mass media and low public participation.[23] Finally, Nancy Fraser challenges Habermas's distinctions between lifeworld and system and material and symbolic reproduction as well as develops an expanded approach to the discussion of need interpretation by introducing a concept that enables the critique of both the ideology and the functional organization of the welfare system: the concept of the ***means of need interpretation.***[24] Hallin's and Fraser's work will be examined more fully in Chapter 7.

Methodological Issues

It is now possible to survey Habermas's choice of method in constructing the *Theory of Communicative Action.* In Habermas's immanent critique, Max Weber, George Herbert Mead, Emile Durkheim, and Alfred Schutz are engaged to provide additional content to Habermas's hypothesis that the learning processes which shape the evolving lifeworld ultimately are governed by the requirements of uncoerced communication. Mead's symbolic interactionism and Durkheim's theory of forms of social solidarity are useful in reconstructing the evolution of communication and forms of social integration—the processes of symbolic reproduction that constitute the lifeworld. Habermas incorporates Mead's reconstructive hypothesis of the genesis of symbolically mediated communication out of the primitive "conversation of gestures," and of the emergence of normatively regulated action: two interacting agents must be capable of recognizing the possibility of a neutral observer's perspective, if they are to recognize that their actions can be governed by norms (*TCA* II, 36). Durkheim's study of the relationship between the evolution of law and forms of group solidarity is applied in support of Habermas's hypothesis that the beginning of sociocultural development occurs in the 'linguistification of the sacred': the replacement of ritual practice with communicative action, of the authority of the holy with the authority of consensus (*TCA* II, 77). To Habermas, then, both Mead and Durkheim illustrate the centrality of developments in communicative practices, and their institutionalization in the rationalization of the lifeworld. However, the distinction between lifeworld and system must be made if the effects on these processes of the nonconsensual, functional organization of society are to be understood.

Alfred Schutz's phenomenological analysis of the lifeworld is employed as a starting point in making this distinction. Habermas is drawn to the work of Alfred Schutz for its thorough phenomenological analysis of the lifeworld as a learned "context of relevance" or background of variously significant elements and events, in which agents locate themselves. However, Schutz is found to be caught within the 'subject-object' framework of the philosophy of consciousness, incapable of making sense of how one of the most basic features of the lifeworld, its intersubjectivity, is possible. A communication-theoretic analysis of the lifeworld, incorporating Mead's and Durkheim's insights concerning the role of communication and language in individual and group identity formation, fares better. Finally, Talcott Parsons furnishes the concept of a functionally defined system. The functional explanations of systems theory, however, are incapable of explaining the consensual processes within which individuals and groups find their identity, interpret their needs and interests, and identify their normative expectations.

The upshot of this discussion for the Habermas's methodological view, then, is that any theory that claims to explain the evolution of modern society must employ the dual method described in the preceding sections. That is, it must recognize in the evolution of modern society the role of two distinct and interacting spheres of development: the (communicative) rationalization of the lifeworld, and the (purposively rational) functional integration of the economic and administrative system. In the remainder of this section, I shall briefly sketch Habermas's reasons for believing that the positions that he discusses in the *Theory of Communicative Action* are insufficient as independent paradigms for social scientific research.

The positions are grouped under three headings: theories of structural differentiation (in the tradition of Max Weber), systems-theoretic approaches (typified by Parsons), and action-theoretical approaches (exemplified by *verstehenden* or interpretive sociology). Habermas finds that the one-sidedness of each of these approaches results in an inability to reveal the "pathologies of modernity." Each of them lacks the range of conceptual resources necessary to distinguish among (1) the structural differentiation of the lifeworld, (2) the autonomous differentiation of action systems, and (3) the interaction between lifeworld and system in the colonization of the lifeworld (*TCA* II, 376–377).

The theory of structural differentiation is principally a historical approach to the evolution of society, in the tradition of Max Weber. For Weber, societal rationalization is a process of the structural differentiation of world-views—the differentiation of 'value spheres' or conceptual domains, and corresponding 'cultural systems of action,' or patterns of activity motivated by interests in the products that are made possible by the use of these conceptual domains.

The value spheres are science and technology, art and literature, and law and morality; the corresponding systems of action are scientific enterprise (conducted in universities), artistic enterprise, the legal system, and the religious congregation. Where in the mythical world-views of primitive cultures these value spheres and systems of action are undifferentiated, the modern world-view is highly differentiated. Ironically, for Weber, this very differentiation has engendered a conflict between the practice of a religiously based ethic of brotherhood and the other systems of action (principally the legal system, scientific enterprise and technology), with which it is incompatible. The inexorable progress of society toward ever more control over nature ultimately reduces the significance of the ethic of brotherliness, as the activities of individuals increasingly are organized for the pursuit of systemic ends, such as economic growth and stability. The rationalization of society, then, leads to a 'loss of meaning' as collectively shared convictions disappear and to a 'loss of freedom' as individual activity increasingly is regulated by bureaucracy.

For Habermas, the principal source of difficulty with Weber's theory lies in (1) its equation of *societal* rationalization with the *functional* rationalization of the economy and the state, and (2) its assumption that ethical commitments can be grounded only in religious commitments and thus themselves are not capable of undergoing rationalization. Although Habermas agrees that the economic and administrative systems integrate activity for functional ends through ethically neutral regulation, ethical commitments are sustained within the lifeworld, in his view, by the communicatively rational appeal to the validity basis of speech. Weber's analysis of the crisis faced by modern society in its inevitable loss of meaning, then, is due to the insufficient scope of his concept of rationality. Weber's 'thesis of the loss of freedom' requires modification, because it is not societal rationalization in itself that results in inappropriate bureaucratic constraints on freedom, but one-sided rationalization.

Habermas frames his criticisms of the early Frankfurt School theorists Theodor Adorno and Max Horkheimer in a similar way. Their "confusion of system rationality with action rationality prevented Horkheimer and Adorno, as it did Weber before them" from distinguishing between the rationalization of the lifeworld and the rationalization of the system. In consequence, their diagnosis of the times locates the possibility of a reconciliation between consciousnesses reified by instrumental reason only in the irrational: "As a result, they could locate the spontaneity that was not yet in the grips of the reifying force of systemic rationalization only in irrational powers—in the charismatic power of the leader or in the mimetic power of art and love" (*TCA* II, 333). For Habermas, of course, reification is the outcome not of rationalization in general, but of the "colonization," by the expansion and differentiation of social systems, of communicatively rational processes.

The second group of theories, based on Parsons' systems theory, will be dealt with below (pp. 103–104).

The third group of theories, classed under what Habermas

calls the *action-theoretic approach,* adopt the point of view of the participant in a society, explaining social structure and change as it appears to one who shares the traditional knowledge, values, and normative expectations inherited by the members of that society. However, theories of the action-theoretic type are intended to reveal more than the character of the individual's assimilation of and accomodation to the society from the subjective point of view. Most important, these accounts are to make intelligible, through the interpretation of shared practices, the nature of collective learning: the means by which societies respond to the contingencies that confront them. The evolving construction of the lifeworld is seen by the action-theoretic approaches as the compound effect of certain basic learning processes. Actions and practices then are explained in terms of their meaning or significance from within these learned world-views. Obviously, then, observers who follow the action-theoretic method are principally interpreters of lifeworlds.

The action-theoretic approach is exemplified by interpretive sociology and takes the view that an adequate understanding of a society can be gained only from the perspective of the participant in that society. Max Weber, Alfred Schutz and G. H. Mead are among the forerunners of the action-theoretic approach, which draws on phenomenology, symbolic interactionism, and hermeneutics. Currently, the action-theoretical approach is employed in interpretive sociological studies that present "modernization processes ... from the viewpoint of the lifeworlds specific to different strata and groups" (*TCA* II, 377). In Habermas's view, such nonhistorical studies not only fail to illuminate the communicative processes underlying broad historical changes in society. They also fail, along with every theory that takes the action-theoretical approach, to account for the effects of the evolving economic and administrative systems on the lifeworld. Though theories taking the action-theoretic approach can contribute to the understanding of lifeworld rationalization, this approach is limited by its inability to account for the emergence of activity premised not on intuitively accessible world-views or a "collective consciousness," but on the ethically neutral requirements of organizations. Because the influences of these organizations are counterintuitive from the lifeworld perspective, the "pathologies of modernity," caused by the colonization of the lifeworld, remain unilluminated and unexplained. "As a result, the subcultural mirrorings in which the sociopathologies of modernity are refracted and reflected retain the subjective and accidental character of *uncomprehended* events" (*TCA* II, 377).

The need for a method that synthesizes the interpretive action-theoretic method with functional analysis essentially is due to the imperfect transparency of the lifeworld from within. Supposing the society were perfectly *transparent* to the lifeworld—that there were a rational explanation that conformed to the norms of communicative rationality for every event or change at the societal level—there would be no need for a counterintuitive explanation that reached beyond the explanations given from within the lifeworld. Habermas identifies three ideal features of such a perfectly transparent lifeworld: the autonomy of the agent, the independence of culture from external forces, and the transparency of communication. (*TCA* II, 148–150) Because, according to Habermas, such an ideal case is actually (though not logically) impossible, actual societies cannot be *explained* from within the lifeworld, they can be only *interpreted.*

First, the presumed autonomy of the agent is a fiction. Agents are never perfectly informed about the situations to which they respond or the consequences and side effects of their actions. Nor are they ever in complete control of the conflicts into which they are drawn or of the possible means to achieve their resolution.

Second, it appears from within the lifeworld as if culture is independent of external forces and conditions: "The lifeworld constitutes, for the action situation, a horizon beyond which it is impossible to venture; it is a totality without a reverse side." For the participants in a lifeworld, "it is utterly senseless to ask whether culture, in the light of which they interact with external nature, society, and inner nature, doesn't really depend, empirically speaking, on *something else.*" However, unintended consequences of actions and other, external, conditions do play a causal role in the transformation of societies and cultures and must be included in an explanation of societal evolution. Thus culture is imperfectly transparent, as the participants' perspective on external nature, society, and inner nature is in each respect imperfectly informed.

Third and most significant, the participant's perspective allows for no stance from which it would be possible to recognize systematic distortion of communication: "resistances that inhere in the structure of the language itself and that severely limit the scope of communication." This feature of the participant's perspective does not, however, rule out the fallibility of that perspective (by making it senseless to ask whether communication is distorted). Hence, communication is not perfectly transparent from the perspective of the lifeworld.

The lack of perfect transparency in the lifeworld is due to the participants' imperfect knowledge and consequent imperfect control of the external constraints on structures and structural changes in the lifeworld. The unintended consequences of their actions, as well as features of their natural environment, affect the content and the limits of the lifeworld in ways invisible from within the lifeworld. Conceiving of the society as a system, on the other hand, allows the theorist to look for explanatory regularities or patterns in the unintended consequences of agents' actions—patterns that can be used to explain developments in the lifeworld.

However, the society also is imperfectly transparent from the external perspective of the observer of the systemic features of society.

> The entities that are to be subsumed under system-theoretic concepts from the external perspective of an observer must be identified beforehand as lifeworlds of social groups and understood in their symbolic structures. The inner logic of the symbolic reproduction of the lifeworld, which we discussed from the standpoints of cultural reproduction, social integration, and socialization, results in *internal limitations* on the reproduction of the societies we view from the outside as a boundary-maintaining system. (*TCA* II, 151)

In particular, Habermas criticizes the assumption that the *origin* of values and norms can be identified within a functionalist theory. Talcott Parsons explains the origin of values by appealing to system goals (or 'control values'): the values that motivate human behavior derive from the goals of the social systems to which they belong. Habermas believes that it is impossible to understand the origin of values and the existence of the normative force possessed by norms that preserve those values without recognizing the existence of a "sphere" of society, the lifeworld, based on commitment to a means of justifying claims about interests and values. The existence of normative force—what motivates commitment to a norm—presupposes either a rational or implicit consensus concerning the *validity* of the norm. But the validity of a norm by its very nature is something determinable only through consensual procedure. Agents' rational or implicit commitments to norms, then, are commitments to consensual positions. For this reason, Habermas argues, agents' values cannot be assumed to be derived from the goals of a social system as a whole: these values originate in the communicative basis of society. Consensus can explain the coherence of personality and society, but the achievement of consensus cannot be explained by system goals. To the contrary, the emergence of system goals assumes the existence of a stable consensual basis for social interactions.

In summary, these methods that Habermas rejects as insufficient are rejected for two kinds of reasons: methodological and critical. That these methods are inadequate given the nature of the subject matter is a methodological claim; that they fail to give a useful diagnosis of the crisis potentials of modern capitalist societies is a specifically critical one.

In the Preface to *The Theory of Communicative Action,* Habermas writes that "alone among the disciplines of social science, sociology has retained its relations to the problems of society as a whole.... As a result, sociology could not, as other disciplines could, shove aside questions of rationalization, redefine them, or cut them down to size" (*TCA* I, 5). Sociology has become the "science of crisis par excellence," a science whose aim of inquiry is to explain "the course of the capitalist modernization of traditional societies and its anomic side effects." In first part of the following chapter, we shall appraise the position of Habermas's project, a product of this "classical" tradition in German sociology, with respect to the expectation of value freedom in social science.

CHAPTER 6

Two Challenges: Positivism and Postmodernism

When his work first began to gather a reputation in this country, Habermas was known principally as an antipositivist. During the 1970s, when the English-speaking world was still being first introduced to Habermas, his name was associated, by philosophers in the analytic tradition, with the cause of antiscientism and methodological dualism (or the view that the methods of the social and natural sciences are fundamentally distinct).[1] The debate between critical theory and neopositivism was brought to a head with the publication of Sir Karl Popper's *The Open Society and Its Enemies,* which assails the method of dialectic explanation employed by Hegel and Marx, the intellectual forebears of the Frankfurt School. The Frankfurt School's critique of instrumental reason, which encompassed a critique of neopositivist epistemology along with mass culture and technocracy, was taken up by Habermas in his early work.[2] Recently, however, Habermas has been concerned more with meeting the challenge of historicism and postmodernism, than with addressing the objections from the neopositivist tradition.

Since the publication in 1981 of the *Theorie des kommunikativen Handlungs,* Habermas's published work has been concerned largely with pleading the cause of modernism, the view that we as a society are and continue to be committed to the ideals of the Enlightenment: freedom, justice, rationality, happiness, social harmony, and, in cultural pursuits, beauty.[3] These essays and lectures are responses to the current 'postmodernist' trend in epistemology, aesthetics, and ethical and political theory. In addition to French 'postmodernism' there is, in the Anglo-American arena, a movement away from the classical and universalist views associated with the Enlightenment and toward a pluralist and tentative understanding of standards of validity or legitimacy, which is skeptical regarding the possibility and even the desirability of an eventual final consensus. In some recent Anglo-American literature (for example, Thomas McCarthy's work), postmodernism in this broader sense has been called the ***new historicism.***[4]

This chapter surveys Habermas's responses to these two competing trends in philosophy and social science: the legacy of positivism, and postmodernism or the new historicism. From neopositivism, the central challenge to Habermas is that the scientific pursuit of value freedom in inquiry is violated by critical theory, which would seem to be an openly value-laden enterprise. In addition to this challenge, advocates of the *verstehenden* approach to social science have been criticized for their adherence to methodological dualism: the view that because the social sciences seek to understand rather than predict or control events in the social world, their methods are fundamentally distinct from those of the natural sciences. In part, this second challenge already has been dealt with in Chapter 5, where it was also pointed out that Habermas has his own criticisms of the *verstehenden* approach. For the rest, Habermas's entire theory of communicative action can be seen as an argument that a predictive and instrumentally useful social science is deeply insufficient as social theory, the pursuit of which must be responsive to the full range of human interests (not merely the interest in manipulating nature).[5]

Habermas's response to the challenges of postmodernism is also a reassessment of modernism and the failures within the tradition of the Enlightenment, which gave rise to postmodernism. Very briefly, his argument is that postmodernist theory itself has not transcended these failures, which are inherent in 'subject-centered' reason and can be overcome only in a theory of communicative reason. I shall return to this argument later in this chapter.

Habermas and the Legacy of Positivism

Habermas's views on the legacy of positivism appear in the rejection of 'scientism' in *Knowledge and Human Interests* (1968), in the discussion of Marcuse in *Towards a Rational Society* (1968), and in the final essay in *Theory and Practice* (1971). Other large issues, however, separate Habermas from the Anglo-American tradition in philosophy, which has its roots in positivism and analytic philosophy of language. The very ideas of a critique of reason or a systematic theory of history by and large are rejected by Anglo-American philosophers and continue to be regarded by many as "speculative philosophy." I have tried to present Habermas's theory in a way that would show that such judgment would be rash. Some rather less crucial, but nonetheless major, points of difference remain between the direction that Habermas envisions for philosophy and social science and the visions that until recently have been dominant on this side of the Atlantic. They revolve around three principal issues:

1. Methodological monism or the view that the natural and social sciences share the same method and aims of inquiry,
2. The value neutrality of natural and social science, and
3. Scientism, or the view that all knowledge is scientific knowledge.

Habermas shares with the *verstehenden* or 'hermeneuticist' view the conviction that social scientific method is distinct from natural scientific method, in that it must seek to understand the significance of actions for the agents who perform them.[6] What distinguishes human scientific from natural scientific method, for Habermas, essentially is the requirement that the human sciences employ a "communicative" method, a method that befits the actual relationship between an interpreter-observer and the participant, who, along with the observer, participates in the ongoing interpretive activity that is social interaction. The observer who is to explain human choices (and not merely human behavior) must become engaged in a dialogue with the subject. This engagement is a special case of the "participant-observation" of modern ethnography and anthropology. Unlike most participant-observation, however, this dialogue is governed by the principles of the ideal speech situation: it is one in which the *validity* claims of both participants are challenged (*TCA* I, 115–116). As a result, the Habermasian participant-observer becomes involved in a 'depth hermeneutical' inquiry governed by the principles of communicative rationality. He or she looks not merely for underlying themes in the structure of interaction, but looks in particular for the reasons for which these themes emerge.

The thesis of methodological dualism characteristically is met with one of two responses: where it is not readily accepted, it tends to be ridiculed. On the one hand, major figures in the philosophy and methodology of social science such as Anthony Giddens, Charles Taylor, and Clifford Geertz have argued for this view, on the basis of the argument that there is a difference between the object domains of the human and natural sciences which, for this reason, demand very different methods.[7] Peter Winch, as a Wittgensteinian, also breaks with the Anglo-American analytic view of the aims of social scientific inquiry.[8] The latter view, often called *methodological monism,* holds that the methods and aims of all of the sciences are fundamentally similar: all the sciences aim to produce, through methodical experimentation and data analysis, an accurate model of reality, distinguished by falsifiable hypotheses, causal generalizations with wide explanatory potential, and predictive accuracy.

It is hardly obvious that an approach that seeks to understand the lifeworld of the subject necessarily excludes the methodical study of controlled cases. Perhaps it would be useful to compare Habermas's method with that of Jean Piaget. Piaget's "clinical" method was certainly communicative; he considered it essential to use whatever verbal or nonverbal means were necessary to identify the particular way that each of his young subjects *understood* his or her experimental tasks. Because of its lack of standardization, his method has met with objections from those who hail from the behaviorist tradition of psychology. Nonetheless, because even the highly "controlled" experiment is subject to differences between the ways in which the various subjects understand the experimental situation, the insufficiency of the noncommunicative method has been acknowledged in some types of research.[9]

A second theme that emerges in the exchanges between the legacy of positivism and critical theory concerns the value neutrality of social science. Each side, traditionally, has accused the other of violating the requirement, though in very different ways. For example, Herbert Marcuse, who popularized critical theory in this country, associated positivism with the ideology of "technocracy" and argued that this ideology is a threat to freedom and community peculiar to modern capitalist states. According to Marcuse, contrary to its own intentions, positivist philosophy of science is laden with the same values pursued by "technological rationality." It is value laden, in his view, because it recommends methods for social science that bias theory-construction in favor of theories that are especially well adapted to the purpose of manipulation.[10]

The standard response from those labeled *positivists* in this dispute has been to point out that any true theory can be used in a variety of ways: it can provide the information needed to determine the means to indefinitely many ends. There is nothing especially well adapted to manipulative purposes about positivist social theory; its use for manipulative purposes is successful just when it is true, but true theories are equally useful for any other purpose. Indeed, many have interpreted critical theory to hold that "positivist" social science is a tool of oppression because it is "all too true." For example, Michael Lessnoff writes that:

> The argument of the critical theorists must be distinguished from a quite different (though perhaps superficially similar) objection to a 'natural science of society,' namely that human beings are inherently free, hence unpredictable, hence inherently unsuited to description in terms of universal deterministic laws. On the contrary, the critical theorists hold, not that such laws predicated of human beings must be untrue, but that they will be all too true, and thus afford to the powerful a weapon for oppressing the rest.[11]

Lessnoff is correct about Marcuse's position, but the passage mischaracterizes Habermas. It is true that Habermas does not believe that human behavior is altogether unpredictable, but he also holds that social scientific theories developed in accordance with a noncommunicative (non-consensus-oriented) method, contrary to the claims of positivism, are not only inherently biased but also *not* "all too true."

Habermas's response to this issue, then, has diverged from those of Marcuse and the early Frankfurt School theorists Theodor Adorno and Max Horkheimer. Where the latter three theorists view positive science as a tool of instrumental reason and an unbridled instrumental reason as the cause of a modern tendency to barbarism, Habermas has tried to point out the limits of instrumental reason in the design of social systems, rather than argue that there is an inherent dominating stance within it.

The polemic image of critical theory casts it as a theory with a leftist political program posing as a theory that reveals hidden truth; in other words, as a value-biased theory. Like most polemical images, the mischaracterization in this image lies more in the assumptions made about the alternative (in this case value-free theories) than in the properties it ascribes to its object. As many social theorists and social scientists point out, the relationship between values and social inquiry is not one that presents a simple choice between two types of theories: value free and value laden.[12] It is not clear, for example, that the results of a research project conducted by "disinterested" observers are straightforwardly value free if the assumptions about what questions those results answer are not. For one thing, reports of results often do not make explicit the distinction between features of the "context of discovery," which are technically irrelevant to the "context of justification." In many cases, this is due to the great complexity of the relationship between context of discovery and context of justification; in others, it is due also to political motives. For example, government funding of research into the social causes of mental illness was discouraged by the administration under former President Reagan, which preferred that scientists look for genetic and neurophysiological causes.[13] At the heart of this official position on government-funded research was the belief that research into social problems in general is value biased. Though the question, What causes mental illness? may sound politically benign, the same question, slightly rephrased as, Whose *fault* is mental illness—genes or unemployment? carries a great deal of political significance. Even though both the "genetic" and the "social causes" research paradigms are welcome from an impartial perspective, the scientific successes of either paradigm can be used by some as reasons *not* to do research of the other kind. But value freedom requires that all available and plausible hypotheses be considered. Although we can never make sure that we are covering all of the possible angles on a given phenomenon and thus can never achieve value freedom in an absolute sense, in principle we can avoid discounting alternative hypotheses without sufficient reason. However, in practice, even this basic requirement of value freedom is extremely difficult to fulfill.

Critical theories are consciously "value laden," but attempt to be so in an impartial way (that is, in a way premised on interests common to all). They are intended to reveal the *telos* of society, which, they assume, always is anticipated in present society. For Habermas, this *telos* is the end of coercion and the attainment of autonomy through reason, the end of alienation through a consensual harmony of interests, and the end of injustice and poverty through the rational administration of justice. However, critical theories do more than merely state our aims as an evolving society. They are supposed to thereby provide a normative basis for the analysis and evaluation of our practices and institutions, which enables us to decide whether they are in our true interests. Habermas has attempted to found this normative basis in a theory of rationality, or an account of the norms to which anyone would have to be committed if he or she were rational.

It might be helpful here to recall again that the German *Sozialwissenschaften* began with the attempt to come to grips with the modern loss of tradition, and the aimlessness it entailed, by understanding *why* modern society had evolved in the first place. The kind of understanding that German sociology from Weber through Habermas has sought, as we have seen, is not modeled on the ideal natural scientific theory, of which Newtonian mechanics has so long been given as the paradigmatic example. But Habermas and others believe that the view, which he calls *scientism,* is prejudicial: namely the view that hypotheses of in the Newtonian tradition of the physical sciences are not only the ideal kind of scientific theory, but also all that can hope to attain the status of knowledge.[14] The major points of difference between Habermas and scientism are two. Habermas believes that scientism unjustly privileges "noncommunicative" over "communicative" inquiry and nomological over reconstructive explanation in social theory. I shall briefly explain each of these differences.

Some "noncommunicative" modes of social scientific inquiry, Habermas argues, pose as objective, impartial methods, while taking basic normative assumptions for granted. For example, economics is premised on the assumption that human beings are utility maximizers *simpliciter.* However, hypotheses of this kind are little more than hypothetical conditionals, which ignore the contribution of communicative processes to the formation of conceptions of the 'good life' ('utility').[15]

A second objection to noncommunicative method concerns its implicit claim to the possibility of unbiased observation or accurate classification of data. Perfectly unbiased observation of course is widely acknowledged to be a fiction. However, it still is expected that, like all scientifically sanctioned properties, all of the scientifically relevant properties of human subjects are observational properties in the standard sense: observable independent of the participant's circumstances or views. For Habermas, this privileging of "noncommunicative" observation not only entails that the observer becomes blind to the role of social interaction in self-definition, it excludes the possibility of knowledge of interests that can be discovered only in an understanding-oriented situation, through communication. If there are such interests, theories about human motivation and action premised on the fiction of pure observation would exclude relevant information as a matter of principle and, therefore, would bias the evidence. Habermas thus implies that a noncommunicative method would hinder, rather than help, the attempt to achieve value neutrality in social theory.[16]

The explanations provided by a social scientific theory must determine motive preferences, dispositions, or interests to explain actions. Because these are not identified through communicative means when the method is noncommunicative, they must be discovered in some other way. In general, they are determined as "revealed preferences." That is, they are "revealed" by looking at patterns of choice such as voting, courting, investment, and consumption. The acceptance of a theory intended to explain behavior as a product of revealed preferences involves the acceptance of the implicit assumption that revealed preferences exhaust *all* the preferences or interests that would be relevant to the explanation of the participant's behavior. But to accept this is to assume that there are no interests that can be understood only by participating in rational discourse. For Habermas, this assumption is unwarranted, given that personal identity is not prior to the social identity we attain by our participation in the communicative processes of the lifeworld.

Habermas believes that the misleading dichotomy between facts and values and the "revealed preferences" (decisionist) interpretation of interests and values themselves are products of one-sided rationalization.[17] Although many of the decisions that affect our social structure are now made by experts of various kinds (for example, medical, industrial relations, urban planning), experts are not recognized as having the authority to decide questions of value. The problem is not that such questions have no answers, but that an essentially collective process has been increasingly individualized and thereby eliminated, and value questions have been rendered into technical questions.[18]

A second difference between Habermas's position and scientism arises from the expectation of scientism that the ideal scientific hypotheses share the logical structure of Newtonian mechanics: a small set of "laws" of immense explanatory power; that is, with deductive relationships to a very large set of observations. It is not logically impossible that a reconstructive theory like Habermas's should have this structure. To make use once again of the parallels between Habermas's and Piaget's reconstructive theories, in principle it is possible that Piaget's few elegant central hypotheses about cognitive development (for example, that cognitive development is a process of assimilation and accomodation) could be specified sufficiently to assume the role of "laws," from which, along with descriptions of initial cognitive capacities and stages of brain development, evolving cognitive structures could be deduced. Habermas's analysis of the norms of rationality might produce a general hypothesis of like structure. His theory could also quite naturally be compared to Marx's theory of history, which some have attempted to recast as a scientific theory also based on the postulation of rationality.[19] Of course, the science of economics has long employed the norms of rationality in something like the role of natural laws, whether to explain long-term historical developments or short-term trends.[20]

It would be a mistake to think of Habermas as antiscientific. Habermas's vision of the relationship between critical theory and the social sciences is a collaborative one. Interestingly, Habermas has made some attempts to integrate his views with those of research developmental psychologists such as Piaget and Kohlberg as well as with other sociological and economic analyses of history, such as those of Weber and Marx. However, he has never been seriously interested in pursuing the "scientistic" end of formulating a testable general hypothesis, principally because the theory of rationality is intended not only to explain societal evolution, but also to provide the basis, with the help of that explanation, for societal self-critique. It is far less important to him to map out ways in which his theory of rationalization could be made compatible with the aims of science in the positivist tradition, than to contribute a means of understanding and evaluating postindustrial welfare society.

Recently, Habermas's most conspicuous critics have come from an entirely different front. The philosophy of postmodernism, as represented by the French writers Jacques Derrida, Michel Foucault, and Jean-François Lyotard, has posed a broad challenge to the philosophy of the Enlightenment, or 'modernism.' Habermas's 'critique of reason,' of course, is firmly rooted in the tradition of the Enlightenment, whose chief end customarily has been understood as the liberation of the individual, by ending superstition and inaugurating a *modern* society, whose institutions are grounded on a principle of justice. For the critics of the Enlightenment, the attempt to ground a theory of society in a theory of rationality to show the way to liberation is destined to failure, as such a theory can only introduce new forms of domination of its own (*PDM,* 56). As Habermas shows, this challenge has roots in a "counterdiscourse" as old as modernity itself.

The Defense of Modernism

Habermas's response to postmodernism is developed in *The Philosophical Discourse of Modernity,* which was published in 1985 and appeared in English in 1987. In *The Philosophical Discourse of Modernity* (1985) Habermas develops most fully the distinction between communicative and 'subject-centered' reason. This distinction, more than anything else, is at the root of what differentiates Habermas's theory of society from that of Marx, his theory of rationality from that of Hegel, and his theory of morality from that of Kant. However, in his preceding works, his attention had been devoted principally to articulating the foundations of the theory of communicative rationality and developing it in the context of a theory of society. The *Theory of Communicative Action,* which draws together the work of a dozen years, develops an analysis of the postindustrial welfare society from the synthesis of the theory of communicative rationality with a reconstruction of historical materialism. The *Discourse* is an extended argument for the claim that most deeply characterizes Habermas's work: that reason is inherently communicative. In what respect, then, does such an argument constitute a defense of modernism against the challenges of postmodernism? Here is the short answer: the theory of communicative rationality provides a resolution to "the problem of modernity," whereas the counterdiscourse of modernity, including postmodernism, does not. The long answer leads through the history of the philosophy of the subject—the critique of subject-centered reason—to the postmodernist rejection of reason. Habermas points to missed opportunities, in the work of Hegel, Marx, Heidegger, and others, to abandon the subject-centered conception for a communicative conception of rationality. These missed opportunities, he argues, have opened the way to postmodernism.

Habermas encapsulates the "problem of modernity" in the following way (It should be noted that not all of the philosophers about whom he writes would concur with this description): "Since the close of the eighteenth century, the discourse of modernity has had a single theme under ever new titles: the weakening of the forces of social bonding, privatization, and diremption—in short, the deformations of a one-sidedly rationalized everyday praxis which evoke the need for something equivalent to the unifying power of religion" (*PDM,* 139). The problem of modernity is an effect, ironically, of what is regarded as the greatest achievement of modern society: the realization of subjective freedom in the economy, the state, and the private and public spheres of discourse. Granting the value of these achievements, however, such individual freedoms also place individuals in conflict with each other, and to complicate matters further, the institutions and 'spheres of life' in which these freedoms are exercised are fragmented—that is, governed by distinct, and self-enclosed, normative foundations. The freedom of the economic agent to pursue his (and later, her) own interests is secured by civil law; freedom as a citizen is guaranteed by the equality of rights, as a private individual by ethical autonomy, and as a public individual by the norms of cultural reflection. Religion, which once had provided a common normative basis for the integration of society, has been superceded by the rationalization and differentiation of the economy, the state, private life, and public life, and its power to express the unity and totality of ethical life is lost:

> In the process, the spheres in which the individual led his life as *bourgeois, citoyen,* and *homme* thereby grew ever further apart from one another and became self-sufficient. This separation and self-sufficiency, which, considered from the standpoint of philosophy of history, paved the way for emancipation of age-old dependencies, were experienced at the same time as abstraction, as alienation from the totality of an ethical context of life. Once religion had been the unbreakable seal on this totality; it is not by chance that this seal has been broken. (*PDM,* 83–84)

The breaking of religion's "unbreakable seal" has brought with it liberation from dependence on superstition, at the price of societal disintegration. The same differentiation of society's normative foundations that breaks the hold of tradition, then, also poses a threat to the genuine liberation and self-realization that it has won.

Although it is in Kant's three critiques (*The Critique of Pure Reason, The Critique of Practical Reason,* and *The Critique of Aesthetic Judgment*) that the differentiation of reason, and the articulation of modern self-understanding, first appears, the problem of modernity was first grasped by Hegel (*PDM,* 16). The philosophical analysis of the conditions of consciousness or 'philosophy of the subject,' begun with Descartes and brought to maturity in Kant's Copernican revolution, was presented by Hegel with the task of addressing a problem in human history: the grounding and unification of a self-consciousness that in the modern age had lost its ties to tradition and had been fragmented by the differentiation of society.[21] Hegel recognized that the lost unity of the subject must be restored, if there were to be any normative foundations for human activity in the future. The question that ultimately had to be answered, for Hegel, was, What is the ideal society, understood as a totality? This question would appear to call for a new normative foundation: one on the basis of which the normatively distinct dimensions of modern society could together be grasped with critical distance (cf. *PDM,* 20). Reason itself, whose nature Hegel believes is incompletely understood by Kant, was made the basis of this critique of the modern subject and its products, a critique that initiated the "dialectic of the Enlightenment." Habermas summarizes the problem of modernity as it appears to Hegel, and the solution that Hegel saw, as follows: "An unprecedented modernity, open to the future, anxious for novelty, can only fashion its criteria out of itself. The only source of normativity that presents itself is the principle of subjectivity from which the very time-consciousness of modernity arose. The philosophy of reflection, which issues from the basic fact of self-consciousness, conceptualizes this principle" (*PDM,* 41).

For Hegel, the "infinite" (and therefore most purely critical) moment of reason is not a mere capacity for negation, but a capacity for reconciling ("sublating" or *Aufheben*)[22] that which has come into opposition, has been lost or sundered. For example, the ethical totality to be regained was conceived by Hegel as a reconciliation ("sublation") within the subject of the individual's self-interested particularity in everyday life with the ethical universal (the moral law), which appears in the rational institutional order of the modern state.[23] What for Kant were "commands of reason" do not have this power for reconciliation; on the contrary, they fix humanity and nature as objects external to the subject, without the capacity for answering and being answered by the opposing element. The abstract moral law, to continue the example, cannot itself restore the ethical totality of life. A reason capable of such a reconciliation must be capable of producing the means of understanding both opposing elements at once. The loss of the "totality of an ethical context of life," brought about by the loss of the unifying power of religion, thus inspired for Hegel a concept of reason as the "reconciling self-knowledge of an absolute spirit" (*PDM,* 84).

Habermas does not believe it is possible to derive a conception of reason capable of providing the normative foundations of a distinctly modern vision of the good society from the nature of subjectivity alone. The central argument developed in the *Philosophical Discourse of the Modern* as indicated earlier is that reason cannot be understood when conceived as subject-centered reason, because it is inherently communicative. This misunderstanding of reason, for Habermas, has entailed both the failures of the Enlightenment to which the counterdiscourse of modernity have drawn our attention, and those of the counterdiscourse itself.

The origins of the current postmodernist assault on modernity are as old as the awareness of the problem of modernity, which makes its first definitive appearance in Hegel. Hegel's attempted solution in the conception of the absolute subject immediately struck many as unsatisfactory. The critics of Hegel's solution to the "problem of modernity" include the Romantics (for example, Schiller, Schlegel), the Left and Right Hegelians (for example, Feuerbach and Rosenkranz, respectively), Karl Marx, and later, Friedrich Nietzsche, and Theodor Adorno and Max Horkheimer. Habermas follows the attempts of Hegel's first critics to provide a solution to the problem of modernity by reworking the philosophy of the subject, through to postmodernism's attempt at repudiating the philosophy of the subject altogether. Nietzsche is a turning point, after which the "problem of modernity" no longer is to be resolved with adjustments to the Enlightenment's conception of reason, but through a repudiation or 'deconstruction' of the very problem of modernity itself, by rejecting the Enlightenment's commitment to reason. Although arguing that postmodernism's rejection of reason in general (rather than subject-centered reason specifically) and its embrace of the 'other of reason' are misguided, Habermas wishes to "resume once again the counterdiscourse that accompanied modernity from the beginning," directing us "toward a *different* way out of the philosophy of the subject" (*PDM,* 301): the shift to a communicative conception of reason. Habermas argues that the philosophy of the subject, with its subject-centered conception of reason, fails to provide the means for reconciling the divisions found in modern societies because of inherent limitations in the philosophy of the subject itself, rather than any limitations entailed by the Enlightenment's commitment to rationality.

The 'counterdiscourse' of modernity (to which Habermas also refers as the 'discourse of modernity') began, with the Left and Right Hegelians and the Romanticists, as attempts to find less remote and ideal means than Hegel's for understanding and overcoming the divisions in modern society: divisions between private individuals, between the particular individual of economic life and the 'universal' and law-governed individual of political life. Hegel had to rely on the conception of the absolute subject alone as the deliverer of reconciliation, effectively removing the possibility of reconciliation far from the complexity and factuality of the actual world. And yet, the absolute subject also held the promise of a *rationally absolute* basis for the good society, something that had to sacrificed in the acceptance of a more modest and desublimated conception of reason.

The Left Hegelians (Habermas speaks of Feuerbach, Marx and Kierkegaard) in particular protest against the sublimation of real conflicts that occurs in Hegel's construal of the problem of modernity and its sublation in the dialectic of Enlightenment. Cast in this general light, this same objection remains alive in the most recent developments of the counterdiscourse: "In the discourse of modernity, the accusers raise an objection that has not substantially changed from Hegel and Marx down to Nietzsche and Heidegger, from Bataille and Lacan to Foucault and Derrida. The accusation is aimed against a reason grounded in the principle of subjectivity. And it states that this reason denounces and undermines all unconcealed forms of suppression and exploitation, of degradation and alienation, only to set up in their place the unassailable domination of rationality" (*PDM,* 55–56). In Marxian materialism, the problem of modernity is not conceived as a conflict between the particularistic individual of civil society and the universal, or as the loss of the "unifying power of religion," as it is by Hegel, but as a conflict between classes, produced by the rational progression of the forces of production, to be transcended only through the reappropriation, by the worker, of alienated socioeconomic power.

Habermas understands Marx as a "variant of the philosophy of the subject that locates reason in the purposive rationality of the acting subject instead of in the reflection of the knowing subject" (*PDM,* 65). However, as Habermas argues, the laborer's reappropriation of the product cannot bring about his or her self-realization of the laborer (that is, end the laborer's self-alienation) if reason is construed only as purposive rationality. If the laborer also *externalizes* himself or herself in the act of production and does not merely produce for practical or material ends, then the activity of producers must be guided by a rationality that is more than purposive rationality; perhaps aesthetic rationality. The norm of purposive rationality is not part of the normative basis of culture (theoretical, ethical-legal, and aesthetic knowledge), and culture, if anything, *just is* the means of individual and collective self-realization. If all reasoning is instrumental, self-realization is impossible. For this reason, Habermas argues, Marx must rely on his early assimilation of labor to artistic creation, if his concept of labor is to provide the normative content necessary for a critique (*PDM,* 64). However, as Habermas points out, this romanticization of labor introduces an ambiguity into the central concept of Marx's theory of modern society. Bereft of any normative guide, the ends toward which productive and technological advance would be aimed are entirely unclear. In addition, Marx's reliance on the abolition of alienated labor (and the abolition of the relations of production) as the means of overcoming alienation requires an unlikely reversal of the differentiation of society (*PDM,* 67).

The Right Hegelians (Karl Rosenkranz and H. F. W. Hinrichs), in contrast to the Left, intended with Hegel to restore the unifying power of religion by means of reflective reason. Unlike Hegel, however, they rejected the need for the absolute subject, and focused their concern on resolving actual tensions in the Weimar Republic. They alleged that acquiescence to the objective rationality of the state and, to provide motivation, the revitalization of tradition are sufficient to compensate for the antagonisms in civil society (*PDM,* 70–73). In short, then, the Right Hegelians rely heavily on the authority of the state, enforced partly through a strong commitment to tradition, to reconcile the perceived conflict of interests.

Finally, for the Romantic philosopher and composer Schiller, the aesthetic was to provide "the medium for the education of the human race to true political freedom" (*PDM,* 45). The Romanticists (Schiller, Schelling, Schlegel, and to some extent, the young Hegel) held that art, "in the form of a new mythology," would become the modern equivalent of the unifying power of religion (*PDM,* 89, 306). For Schelling, this capacity of art derives from its power to reveal the form not only of the beautiful, but also of the good and the true; for Schlegel, it is derived from poetry's special "divinatory gift," distinct from philosophy, science, and ethics. The Romantic call for a new poetic mythology anticipates Wagner's and Nietzsche's emphasis on the potential of art, as revived mythology, to restore the experience of unity. The Romantic elevation of the aesthetic experience to a power of reconciliation anticipates Adorno's appeal to the reconciliatory potential of the aesthetic in his critique of modernity.

Friedrich Nietzsche questioned the capacity of reason conceived as a "religion of culture" (that is, as characterized by the Right Hegelians) to replace the power of mythology to unify the conflicting intentions and motivations of distinct individuals. Because the *motives* underlying the remembered traditions themselves have been lost, these traditions are "contrary to need, no longer . . . impelling to action," and thus limited to the purely inner life of the subject.[24] Rather than attempt yet another revision of the conception of reason to overcome this failure of modernity to fashion its own values, however, Nietzsche chose to step out of the dialectic of Enlightenment altogether. Habermas bills this move as the turning point in the critique of modernity. Here the counterdiscourse of modernity begins in earnest, challenging the liberal self-understanding of modernity. In the place of reason, the counterdiscourse embraces the 'other of reason,' making the entry into postmodernity.

Habermas traces this shift in the discourse of modernity, first undertaken by Nietzsche, to the latter's final loss of confidence in the ability of modernity to "fashion its criteria out of itself" by making adjustments to the notion of reason (*PDM,* 86): "for from ourselves we moderns have nothing at all."[25] Nietzsche turns to pre-Christian archaic culture, but does not urge a reactionary 'return to origins.' The paralyzing time-consciousness of the modern age must not only be be accepted (there is no possibility of a return to an age innocent of history), but "heightened": the myths of the ancient past provide a source of new values, but only for those who see themselves as builders of the future. Myth is the other of reason; specifically, the figure of *Dionysus* is the "shattering of the *principium individuationis,*" the preindividuated self capable of ecstacy.[26] The *Dionysian* is the power to create meaning, which precedes the distinction between true and false, good and evil (*PDM,* 95). Reason is declared to be nothing more than a masked expression of the will to this power. Indeed, it is a perversion of the will to power: in the guise of reason, the will to power creates nihilistic illusions, such as the apparent universal norms produced by reason and the "ascetic ideal." However, the will to power also is capable of taking the affirmative, value-creating stance of the *Dionysian.* For Nietzsche, then, the abstract morality of modernity, and its nihilistic self-understanding in the wake of the death of God, must be overcome, not reassured.

Habermas argues that the basis of Nietzsche's critique of reason is principally aesthetic: "Nietzsche enthrones taste, 'the Yes and No of the palate,' as the organ of knowledge beyond true and false, beyond good and evil" (*PDM,* 96). Furthermore, rather than acknowledge the normative content of aesthetic judgment, and its proximity in this respect to theoretical and ethical reason, Nietzsche simply declares the aesthetic to be the other of reason. In Habermas's view, Nietzsche is on unstable ground, caught between two uncomfortable choices: he can assert the truth of the philosophy of the will to power (in which case, Habermas argues, he would ultimately need to recognize the obligation to defend that claim and abandon his rejection of reason), or he must conduct a critique of metaphysics that somehow shows the whole of metaphysics to be illegitimate, without destroying altogether the possibility of philosophy (and therewith his own views). Habermas finds that Nietzsche's critique of modernity has been carried on in both directions, Nietzsche's influence on Bataille passing to Foucault, that on Heidegger to Derrida. Bataille and Foucault simply presuppose the philosophy of the will to power, and Heidegger and Derrida conduct critiques of metaphysics that "attack its own roots": an immanently conducted destruction and the deconstruction (respectively) of metaphysics.

Georges Bataille discovers in the limit experiences of the sacred and the violent, and Michel Foucault in that which is prohibited and excluded by the modern form of subjectivity, a point of view from which reason and the rationalization of society appear as forms of power. Bataille's close anthropological investigations of limit experiences disclose their ability to transgress and extinguish the purposively rational self, opening the self to the experience of the surreal: "The curious gaze with which Bataille patiently dissects the limit experiences of ritual sacrifice and sexual love is guided and informed by an aesthetics of terror. . . . In these explosive stimuli are joined the countervailing tendencies of longing and of horrified withdrawal into paralyzing fascination. . . . The consciousness exposed to these rending ambivalences enters a sphere beyond comprehension" (*PDM,* 100). This "profane illumination" reveals subversive forces in the human psyche, forces that, according to Bataille, social structure and convention are inherently designed to *exclude.* Like Foucault, who was greatly influenced by him, Bataille does not employ the Freudian model of repression in his analysis of morality and social structure, but draws instead on Nietzsche's analysis of the perversion, by the weak, of the *Dionysian* will to power. As the weak oppose the strong in Nietzsche, society operates on the basis of a principle of "exclusion"; a drawing of boundaries between experiences compatible with day-to-day existence and cooperation in purposive activity, on the one hand, and the sacred or "taboo," on the other. The rationalization and differentiation of society is seen, by Bataille, as the proliferation of boundaries, separating the stimuli of violently erotic and sacred experience from the domain of moral, polite and social existence. Though Bataille was a Marxist, he found that the requirements of productivity alone do not explain the normative force of social norms. Instead, their normative force derives from the force of the simultaneous fascination and repulsion aroused by experiences of a sacred nature. Reason cannot determine the limits of transgression, because these limits are not rational: reason can be exercised only after internal nature has been tranquilized. There therefore is an intimate connection between social prohibitions and the sacred.

> In the beginning, a calm opposition [of prohibitions] against the violence [of internal nature] would not have sufficed to separate the two worlds. If the opposition did not itself have its share of violence, . . . reason alone would not have posessed enough authority to determine the limits of transgression. Only unthinking fear and horror could offer resistance in the face of boundless unbridledness. This is the nature of the taboo: It

> makes possible a world of tranquillity and reason, but is itself and in its very principle in the nature of a shudder that befalls not the intelligence but the spirit.[27]

In Judeo-Christian tradition, however, this connection between prohibition and the sacred that is "the very nature of the taboo" is weakened, because that tradition has expunged the diabolical from the sacred, as part of the process of ethical rationalization (here Bataille borrows from Weber). Nonetheless, Bataille's *General Economics* predicts a final reckoning. Excluded from the modern Protestant morality of frugality and diligence is the possibility of unproductive expenditure and consumption, which, according to Bataille, must occur, if not in the form of glorious, magnanimous *Bacchanalia,* then in the shape of catastrophe: nuclear destruction, military (mis)adventures, and the like.

The positive figure in Bataille's thought—the one who transgresses boundaries, and gloriously squanders his or her wealth of energy—is called a *sovereign,* as Nietzsche's noble man is called *Übermensch.* Habermas points out that it is not clear how this figure, whose power is its charisma and whose charisma derives from its diabolical excess, is distinguishable from the ideal fascist leader, another type of figure that interested Bataille for similar reasons. In keeping with his critique of the counterdiscourse, however, Habermas's principal doubts are directed to what he sees as Bataille's failure to complete a radical critique of reason. The sacred, as the 'other of reason,' incommensurable with reason or the rational subject, cannot contain a critique of reason, nor indeed can it ground Bataille's anthropological investigation of morality (*PDM,* 235–236). Somewhat uncharacteristically, however, Habermas does not develop a direct response to Bataille's analysis of the normative force of social and ethical standards.

Michel Foucault, like Bataille, was a radical critic of reason and societal rationalization. Again like Bataille, he wished to conduct this critique by adopting an alternative approach to history; an approach that recognizes what is excluded by societal rationalization, as well as by the method of historiography itself, and thereby intended to unmask the true nature of rationalization. For Foucault, the emergence of demands for institutional legitimacy, far from dissipating the seats of arbitrary power, ushered in new means for the concentration and exertion of power. There are echoes here of Nietzsche's analysis and reevaluation of Christian morality, in which perceived 'forces of light' are revealed as forces of darkness. However, in Foucault, the relatively simple and valuatively rich distinction between the resentful weak and the noble strong is lost, and instead power becomes entirely impersonal, assuming many historically specific forms whose value is undecided. Since the Enlightenment, power is to be found in the regimentation of the mind and of the body, as is to be witnessed in the themes of Foucault's histories of mental and penal institutions. Against an age that prided itself on its achievement of subjective freedom, Foucault intended to show that the "free" and rational subject of the Enlightenment is the product of a prolific array of disciplinary and penal techniques, instantiated in institutions as diverse as education, medicine, and the workplace, as well as military and penal institutions. Furthermore, Foucault argued that the human sciences, established since the beginning of the age of Modernity (since the end of the eighteenth century), are no more and no less than the sciences of this regimentation.[28] The power and the knowledge of modernity each necessitate the form taken by the other. "*In their very form,* the human sciences are supposed to present an amalgam of knowledge and power; *the formation of power and the formation of knowledge compose an indissoluble unity*" (*PDM,* 272).

However, Habermas finds that this strong claim rests on weak grounds, which manifest an inconsistency in Foucault's analysis of the human sciences. He argues that the way Foucault intended to overcome the philosophy of the subject is inconsistent. Foucault's central concept, that of power, is, according to Habermas, taken from the philosophy of the subject (*PDM,* 274). As Habermas understands it, the philosophy of the subject conceives of the subject as capable of "only two relationships to the world of imaginable and manipulable objects: cognitive relationships regulated by the *truth* of judgments; and practical relationships regulated by the *success* of actions" (*PDM,* 274). But because the success of an action depends on the truth of the judgments made in planning the action, power is dependent on truth. (There must be a subject who knows the truth, for the successful exertion of power to be possible.) Habermas argues that Foucault illicitly reverses this dependence to overcome the philosophy of the subject, asserting truth to be dependent on power (that is, that power introduces the possibility of a distinction between true and false), in his analysis of the human sciences as a technique of domination. If truth is dependent on power, there is no need for the knowing and judging subject in history, which becomes an account of power. But Foucault cannot have it both ways, and if truth is dependent on power, then his own account of history fares as well or as badly as anyone else's; in other words, he risks grounding his account of history on relativism (*PDM,* 276).

Unfortunately, this criticism is inadequately developed, for it fails to address Foucault's theory of the subject as a product of power and the productive theory of power that underlies it. To many readers, it seems clear that Foucault does *not* "borrow" his concept of power "from the philosophy of the subject" (cf. *PDM,* 274), but rather presents a deeply useful alternative to the agent-centered understanding of power. Habermas needs to show an essential connection between power and the subject, if it is to be shown that Foucault must ultimately presuppose such a connection.[29]

A second, more widely recognized, difficulty with Foucault's analysis of power-knowledge is its failure to give any account of its own normative foundations. This criticism is less strained, and possibly more important, than the first, given that Foucault's intent was not merely theoretical, but critical in the general sense of the term. Is *Discipline and Punish* an indictment of the Enlightenment and the power that produced it? If so, then Foucault would have to relinquish his view that "there is no illegitimate power." If not, then how could it reveal anything of importance about the Enlightenment? Habermas notes that, in the process of developing his arguments in writing, Foucault is not consistent about the normative content of his historical accounts.[30] "If one tries to glean the standards implicitly appealed to in his indictments of disciplinary power, one encounters familiar determinations from the normativistic language games that he has explicitly rejected. The asymmetric relationship between powerholders and those subject to power, as well as the reifying effect of technologies of power, which violate the moral and bodily integrity of subjects capable of speech and action, are objectionable for Foucault, too."[31] In fact, there were times when Foucault was stunningly straightforward about his evaluative and normative commitments. An example can be found in the preface to Deleuze and Guattari's *Anti-Oedipus:*

> This art of living counter to all forms of fascism, whether already present or impending, carries with it a certain number of essential principles which I would summarize as follows if I were to make this great book into a manual or guide to everyday life:
>
> - Free political action from all unitary and totalizing paranoia.
> - Develop action, thought, and desires by proliferation, juxtaposition, and disjunction, and not by subdivision and pyramidal hierarchization.
> - Withdraw allegiance from the old categories of the Negative (law, limit, castration, lack, lacuna), which Western thought has so long held sacred as a form of power and an access to reality. Prefer what is positive and multiple, difference over uniformity, flows over unities, mobile arrangements over systems. Believe that what is productive is not sedentary but nomadic.[32]

Here and elsewhere Foucault appears to imply that normative foundations are neither necessary nor desirable, as they lead to "totalizing" or fascist forms of political action. However, one wonders where his own "manual for everyday life" springs from, if not some set of considered normative judgments. Habermas suggests that Foucault may ultimately offer little more than a "relativist self-denial" (*PDM,* 294). If Foucault's intention was to develop a radical critique of reason, then it is unclear from what basis the critical force of such a critique could be derived. If the critique was supposed to succeed by subordinating truth to power, it cannot, for this is mere sleight of hand (*PDM,* 274). Of course, it is at very the core of Habermas's own conception of reason that when 'reason' itself comes to serve arbitrary power, it no longer is reason but manipulation, premised on the distortion of the norms of communicative rationality. Alternatively, when reason brings about the proliferation of offices and procedures that bear no relation to human interests, it is due to the predominance of functional over communicative rationality and the problematic tendency of functional organization to expand even in dysfunctional ways.

Criticisms of Habermas to the effect that he clings to an outmoded "totalizing" form of theory are common, yet I suspect that this criticism often rests on a misconception of Habermas as the prophet of a doctrine for modern society. His model of consensus formation sometimes is perceived as Eurocentric and doctrinaire, in spite of his emphasis on freedom from coercion and the fact that many "nonmodern," non-European societies are run consensually.[33] Habermas is not even a visionary, if to be a visionary is to have a utopian vision. In this respect as in others, Habermas as a contemporary Marxian diverges from Marx. He is, however, troubled by the "the exhaustion of utopian energies," as this is linked to the very breakdown of communication he finds so threatening.[34] Here it is possible to discern a common concern with Foucault.

There is a second path taken by the counterdiscourse of modernity, also leading to the present. Where Bataille and Foucault develop critical perspectives on the rationalized society out of Nietzsche's theory of power, Heidegger and Derrida conduct the radical critique of reason by "attacking the roots of reason" itself to achieve the destruction and deconstruction of metaphysics.

Heidegger's critique of metaphysics is characterized by Habermas as a response to the self-undermining tendencies of Nietzsche's critique of reason as power, which becomes a "temporalized philosophy of origins" (*PDM,* 131). In Heidegger's view, it is possible that the destruction of metaphysics through an immanent and philosophical critique could replace a new mythology as the means of overcoming the loss of commitment to living values that Nietzsche calls *nihilism,* without undermining itself, as Nietzsche's critique threatened to do (*PDM,* 97). Nietzsche's triumph over nihilism through the *Dionysian* thus becomes, in Heidegger, the overthrow of metaphysics through the memory-revelation of Being. Being (as opposed to beings: things, creatures) is an origin, in the sense that it precedes all human understanding and therefore all culture and society. However, Heidegger offers a *temporalized* philosophy of origins, in that it is not simply a call for a return to a pure and historically innocent original state. There is necessarily a history to how Being is understood, which, for Heidegger, amounts to a history of Being itself.

As is now obvious if it was not before, the 'question of Being' is the fundamental one, in Heidegger's philosophy. Heidegger describes the modern state of mental life as a state of "forgetfulness" of Being. This term is potentially misleading: understanding Being is not a matter of jogging the memory or remembering knowledge held before birth, as in Plato's *Meno*. Rather, the possession of a metaphysics is itself the state of forgetfulness of Being, and "remembering" Being is not merely a matter of recall, but of learning how to think all over again. All cultures possess an ontological preunderstanding, constituted of basic concepts that determine the horizons of experience of a culture, although these concepts are not always developed philosophically into a metaphysics. Heidegger speaks of the pre-Socratics, who preceded metaphysics, as inhabiting an "original" state prior to the "abandonment by Being" that occurred with the beginning of metaphysics.

There is also a specifically modern understanding of Being. Accordingly, the problem of modernity assumes a new guise in Heidegger: "That period we call modern . . . is defined by the fact that man becomes the center and measure of all beings. Man is the *subjectum,* that which lies at the bottom of all beings, that is, in modern terms, at the bottom of all objectification and representation."[35] Subject-centered reason, which, since its beginning in Descartes, positions as the ground of being the capacity for thought and experience of the subject, is seen by Heidegger as itself the problem of modernity. This subjectivism itself entails the endless expansion of the power of manipulation—of objectification—that ends in nihilism. It can be overcome by learning *how to think*—and more specifically, by learning how to think in a way that allows Being to "unconceal" itself. That Being should unconceal itself, rather than be discovered by us, appears strange only because of the philosophical prejudices imposed by the subject-object distinction, which posit the discoverable object to the subject's discovery.

Habermas, however, believes that Heidegger obscures rather than overcomes the problem of modernity expressed in Nietzsche's appeal for a new mythology. That appeal, which had arisen out of the "pathologies of an ambigiously rationalized life-world" and the "palpable distortions of everyday communicative practice," is answered not with an analysis of those distortions, but an "enciphering" into "an impalpable destining of Being" (*PDM,* 139). The problem of modernity becomes murky if not unrecognizable in Heidegger. In keeping with the development of the *Discourse of Modernity,* however, Habermas's central criticism of Heidegger is that he fails to fulfill his intention to exit the philosophy of the subject, and the metaphysics produced by it, without undermining his own path or collapsing into mysticism: "Heidegger only escapes the paradoxes of a self-referential critique of reason by claiming a special status for *Andenken* [the thinking of Being], that is, its release from discursive obligations" (*PDM,* 188). "The rhetoric of the later Heidegger compensates for the propositional content that the text itself refuses: It attunes and trains its addresses in their dealings with pseudo-sacral powers" (*PDM,* 140). Although the claims to truth of Western philosophy and science are to be superceded, as they are premised on the forgetfulness of Being, the new truth in their stead—the unconcealment of Being—is mysteriously immune from challenge and above justification. "The luminous force of world-disclosing language is hypostatized" in Heidegger (*PDM,* 154). According to Habermas, Heidegger apparently could overcome subject-centered reason only by depriving truth claims of their character as validity claims altogether: truth claims are no longer to be rationally motivated; truth is simply to "occur." Habermas explains the appearance of this special status claimed for *Andenken* as a response to a "dead end" in *Being and Time,* whose analysis of our awareness of Being (*Dasein*) had to become an analysis of the conditions of subjective experience.[36] This implausible "turn" in Heidegger's philosophy is, to Habermas, also partly explained by Heidegger's identification with, and later attempt to distance himself from, some of the millenialist aims of Nazism (*PDM,* 155–160). In 1933–1934, when he campaigned for and spoke for the National Socialist movement, Heidegger had begun to speak of finding the authenticity of *Dasein* in a collective will, "fused by the Fuhrer," rather than in the existence of the individual. Later, however, the concrete history of the Third Reich becomes "sublimated," according to Habermas, into an unfortunate phase in the history of Being (*PDM,* 159–160).

In the work of Jacques Derrida, the essential thinking that destroys metaphysics (*Andenken*) becomes 'deconstruction,' and Being becomes 'archewriting.' Derrida assimilates the critique of metaphysics to a critique of the authority of the spoken word (a 'grammatology'). The object of his focus and the technique he calls *deconstruction* is a mistaken presumption of the identity of meaning, which occurs as a result of the simultaneous experience of hearing one's own voice speak the word and thinking the intended meaning of the word. This experience entails that "the word is lived as the elementary and undecomposable unity of the signified and the voice, of the concept and a transparent substance of expression."[37] This undecomposable unity of the word, however, is an illusion. If language is approached as written text rather than spoken word, the unique identity of the text's meaning is lost, and the '*differance*' between the signifier (and its possible relations to other signifiers, or the "transparent substance of expression") and the signified (the content of thought, as intended or experienced by the subject) becomes discernible.[38] The '*differance*' between signifiers, whether uttered or written, and the signified is likened to the Heideggerian difference between Being and beings: it is what makes possible meaning and therefore the disclosure of the world. In articulating this idea, Derrida employs Ferdinand de Saussure's intuition that meaning is inherently relational—that it inheres in the 'differences' between signs.

Derrida uses the metaphor of an 'archewriting'—an original, subjectless (authorless) generator of relations between signs, which is *present* to us only in the form of fragmented 'traces'—to describe the world-disclosing capacity of the written text, which is made possible by *differance.* When completely uncoupled from the presumption of unitary meaning, the path taken by the interpretation of written text becomes that of deconstruction: the making visible of *differance.* (This claim should be kept distinct from the claim of the literary critical position called *New Criticism,* that the meaning of a text is independent of all other texts. Derrida denies this.) But if deconstruction's aim is the revelation of *differance,* which, after all, just is the denial of the uniqueness of meaning (though it demands interpretation nonetheless), then deconstruction is the ultimate antithesis of interpretation. The notion of the trace, precisely because it is a central one for Derrida, plays on the meaning of *trace* in psychoanalysis, archeology, paleontology, and other such contexts, which initially would appear to be quite peripheral or marginal to the philosophical content of Derrida's purpose. In Derrida's words, "*The (pure) trace is differance.* ... The trace is in fact the absolute origin of sense in general. Which amounts to saying once again that there is no absolute origin of sense in general. The trace is the difference which opens appearance [*l'apparaître*] and signification."[39] But as is the case with any word, there also is no original sense of the word *trace*. Being, by whose plenitude, for Heidegger, the presence of beings to consciousness is possible, is itself deconstructed in Derrida's work. The presence of beings, and therewith the meaning of language, becomes a trace—mere slippage, which nonetheless demands interpretation:

> Reconciled here to a Heideggerian intention,... [the notion of a trace] signifies, sometimes beyond Heideggerian discourse, the undermining of an ontology which, in its innermost course, has determined the meaning of being as presence and the meaning of language as the full continuity of speech. To make enigmatic what one thinks one understands by the words "proximity," "immediacy," "presence"... is my final intention in this book. This deconstruction of presence accomplishes itself through the deconstruction of consciousness, and therefore through the irreducible notion of the trace (*Spur*), as it appears in both Nietzsche and Freud.[40]

Thus Derrida's critique of metaphysics goes a step beyond Heidegger's: the deconstruction of Being. In Habermas's view, however, this path to the exit from the philosophy of the subject, like Heidegger's, "promotes only a mystification of palpable social pathologies" (*PDM,* 181).

There are also doubts about whether the path is clear at all. For Habermas, everything in Derrida's position depends on whether one thesis can be held, namely, that rhetoric precedes logic—that "serious" language is just a special case of "nonserious" rhetoric. As Jonathan Culler explains Derrida's position with regard to genres, "If serious language is a special case of nonserious, if truths are fictions whose fictionality has been forgotten, then literature is not a deviant, parasitical instance of language. On the contrary, other discourses can be seen as cases of a generalized literature, or archi-literature."[41] Derrida intends in the practice of deconstruction to eliminate the distinction between literature and philosophy, or indeed, between any literary genres (*PDM,* 190). According to Derrida's grammatology, the rhetorical and infinitely reinterpretable content of the *written* text far exceeds the intended (and, in the case of philosophy, rationally developed or "logical") content of the author's *spoken* words, and so much so that it is possible to interpret the written text in such a way that it openly contradicts the author's intended meaning. Because the text itself imposes no constraints on what is "marginal" and what is "central" to the meaning it holds, anything is fair in constructing such a deconstructive interpretation. In short, philosophy is indistinguishable from fiction.

Habermas argues that this leveling of the distinction between literature and philosophy cannot be made without self-contradiction. Derrida's reversal of the priority of nonliterary over literary discourse entails that "literal" meaning is just a certain kind of play on "nonliteral" meaning. But Habermas argues that communication is not possible unless "nonliteral" meaning and fictional discourse is derivative of literal, or "serious," meaning, which has the status of literal meaning simply because it is tied to the validity basis of speech (*PDM,* 194–199). The argument is similar to the one discussed in Chapter 3 of this book. Metaphysics cannot then be deconstructed if that involves discarding the discursive obligations of the validity basis of speech, for that attempt must undermine itself by destroying meaning. According to Habermas, literary discourse is neither entirely autonomous from, nor indistinguishable from, nonliterary discourse. Rather, in literature, the normative force of the validity basis of speech is suspended (in other words, illocutionary force is suspended), though the fact that the suspended validity claims imitate those made in everyday communication is instrumental in our ability to understand literary language (*PDM,* 199–204). But if literature does not raise and defend validity claims, then it is unclear how the techniques of *literary* criticism could render *philosophical* texts (which, after all, do raise and defend validity claims) "accessible in their essential contents." The priority of nonliterary over literary discourse also is apparent in everyday communicative practice.

Without collective recognition of the validity basis of speech, no cooperative planning of action could be undertaken.

The challenge to the assumption that there are such things as literal meanings may be Derrida's most important contribution to philosophy. A similar challenge was made by Wittgenstein, in his 'private language argument.'[42] Habermas has not fully answered this challenge, as his response amounts to little more than an assertion of the necessity of the validity basis of speech. However, his own challenge to any possible theory of communication, that it explain the possibility of mutual understanding (the basis of all cooperation), is at least equally compelling.

Finally, one cannot forget Theodor Adorno and Max Horkheimer, who, rather than "gather under Nietzsche's banner" as did Heidegger and Bataille, do "battle with Nietzsche" (*PDM*, 131). Nietzsche's appeal to a new mythology, and his repudiation of reason as the source of nihilism, is metamorphosed in Adorno and Horkheimer's *Dialectic of Enlightenment* into a critique of the Enlightenment *as* mythology: "Myth is already enlightenment; and enlightenment reverts to mythology ... the difference as well as the unity of mythic nature and enlightened mastery of nature" appear in the rituals, shared by mythology and the Enlightenment, of sacrifice and renunciation.[43] The mythology of the Enlightenment is grounded in the subject-object division peculiar to the philosophy of the subject: "The permanent sign of the enlightenment is domination over an objectified external nature and a repressed internal nature."[44] To gain autonomy, a subject-centered reason must divorce itself from the 'other' (traditionally, nature and human nature) that is its object. However, this divorce of subject and object itself is problematic, because it introduces an illusion of subjective autonomy, at the expense of objectifying all else into what can be dominated by the subject. This domination is the expression of an inherent self-destructiveness in reason, which results from its tendency to spawn divisions, and leads to totalitarianism and barbarism: "Enlightenment is totalitarian."[45] Habermas expresses doubts about the ability of Adorno and Horkheimer to save this critique of reason from performative contradiction by merely "eschewing theory" and practicing the "determinate negation" of the fusion of reason and power (*PDM*, 128). Adorno's flight into the aesthetic also raises doubts.

One of the minor themes of *The Discourse of Modernity* concerns the potential of art to perform the reconciliation of the divisions wrought by modernity. The possibility is raised by Hegel and the Romanticists, by Nietzsche and Adorno. In and after Nietzsche, the aesthetic appears principally as the 'other of reason,' which offers a domain in which that reconciliation could be found. Habermas himself, of course, believes that aesthetic reflection is possible—that aesthetic expression raises a validity claim about its own authenticity. Thus the aesthetic, for Habermas, is neither Nietzsche's prerational Dionysus nor Adorno's nonrational mimesis. Nor is it even Schiller's source of an aesthetic unity between the distinct demands of material reproduction and moral life. For Habermas, the reconciliatory potential of art is not found in any capacity that it has for *negating* our commitment to the norms of rationality or even for reconciling distinct domains of communicative rationality, but rather in the contributions that its creative discovery of new forms of experience makes to social life. Habermas remains, on the whole, closer to the classical view of the aesthetic as a place to explore possible harmonies of interests.

The question of how to understand the aesthetic is another point of contention between Habermas and the postmodernists. The reconciliatory and harmonizing potential of art, which Aristotle was perhaps the first to attempt to explain, is the theme of Kant's analysis of beauty in the *Critique of Judgment.* On this view, derived from Kant, aesthetic experience becomes the place where possible harmony of interests can be explored, without the constraints of factual reality or obligation. The French postmodernist Jean François Lyotard would prefer to advance the avant-garde's pursuit of the sublime experience—the experience of the impossibility of harmony—to the modernist's aesthetic experience as the experience of reconciliation and harmony of interest.[46] Though Lyotard's analysis of the sublime also is rooted in Kant, the ideal of beauty (as it is understood by Kant) lies closer to the ideals of the Enlightenment tradition. Lyotard has asserted that Habermas's ideally consensual society expresses an aesthetic of beauty, but it is difficult to fit the latter's position so neatly into that category, unless one has quite an oversimplified and saccharine picture of how a society whose institutions were based on consensus would carry on.[47] The requirement of the ideal speech situation that all participants receive equal opportunity to present their views is more than compatible with an interest in ending the suppression of diversity, aesthetic or otherwise—and that requirement quite outstrips existing practice in any existing democracy. Aesthetics that radically challenge existing culture, then, are quite compatible with Habermas's conception of democracy, unless they entail injustice. It is not clear that any of the postmodern theorists have succeeded in challenging the deeper commitment behind Habermas's theory of rationality: the end of coercion.

The position developed in the *Philosophical Discourse of Modernity* is brought together in the following passage: "If it should turn out that [the challenge to modernity] does not seriously lead beyond the philosophy of the subject, we would have to return to the alternative that Hegel left in the lurch back in Jena—to a concept of communicative reason that places the dialectic of the enlightenment in a different light. Perhaps the discourse of modernity took the wrong turn at that first crossroads" (*PDM,* 74). All attempts to "lead beyond the philosophy of the subject" by embracing the 'other' of reason, or by attacking the roots of the critique of subject-centered reason itself, Habermas argues, must fail. The 'other' of reason, whether it be the aesthetic, the Dionysian, or power, contains insufficient normative force to sustain a critique of reason. An attack on the roots of critique itself, moreover, can lead only to a performative contradiction. The philosophy of the subject, including its flight to the 'other of reason,' is inherently flawed: it assumes that the constitution of the subject precedes communication, and the claims to truth and normative validity that are intersubjectively established in communication. Any attempt at a critique of reason that leaves this assumption intact, seeking a basis for subjective freedom and social harmony "beyond" the norms of communication, is bound to fail.

Because these attempts at abandoning subject-centered reason cannot, without contradiction, be sustained by normative foundations, it follows that they are also unable to support a *critical* theory. For Habermas, the repudiation of the validity basis of communication does not lead the way out of the self-destructive tendencies in a one-sidedly rationalized society, but further into them. It is Habermas's conviction that the replacement of communicative with functional reason, and the power of the functional demands of the system to replace the validity basis of speech, is the true object of the critique of modernity. Functional or systemic constraints, appearing in the form of ideology (for example, social Darwinism), rather than the constraints of (communicative) reason, constitute the 'will to power' in modern society.

> The idea that the capacity to compete on an international scale—whether in markets or in outer space—is indispensible for our very survival is one of those everyday certitudes in which systemic constraints are condensed. Each one justifies the expansion and intensification of the forces of the others, as if it were not the ground rules of social Darwinism that are at the bottom of the play of forces. Modern Europe has created the spiritual presuppositions and the material foundations for a world in which this mentality has taken the place of reason. That is the real heart of the critique of reason since Nietzsche. (*PDM*, 366–367)

Habermas's *Discourse* can be seen in a broader light as offering a response to what has been called the *new historicism*—generally, the epistemological position shared by the postmodernists and those who are receptive to postmodern philosophy in the United States—which questions the ability of philosophy to answer the core questions of the Western philosophical tradition. These core questions are about the nature of reason, truth, and the good, and those values that have been held to be part of the good: freedom, happiness, and virtue. The principal hallmark of the new historicism is the denial of the existence of unique and universal standards of truth and normative validity, as well as of the validity of philosophical attempts to determine such standards. Richard Rorty challenges the ability of philosophy to provide "foundations" for knowledge, indeed, to make anything more than tautologous statements about truth.[48] There are philosophical alternatives to both foundationalism and the new historicism, of course, as a recent volume on the "end of philosophy" is concerned to illustrate.[49] The contributions to *After Philosophy: End or Transformation?* contrast the "end of philosophy" theorists

(Lyotard, Foucault, Derrida and Rorty's position in *The Consequences of Pragmatism*) with the nonfoundationalist and nonrelativist 'transformative' responses of other philosophers, such as Michael Dummett, Habermas, and Alasdair MacIntyre. Habermas's consensus theory, then, is only one of several attempts to identify the sense of 'truth' and 'normative validity' in a way that draws on the purposes for which we use these terms, without paying homage to transcendental foundations. Against the "end of philosophy" theorists, Habermas defends the role of modern philosophy as the "guardian of reason"; as the "placeholder" and not the arbiter for future consensus and the means of achieving consensus in science, morality and art.[50]

It is also possible to argue that the 'foundationalism' issue is a bit of a red herring. The question of whether one should or should not accept a theory of justification ought not to be decided independently of what *sort* of theory of justification is being talked about. The theory of communicative rationality, then, ought not stand or fall on the basis of whether it is a 'foundationalist' theory. More important, however, too much of the discussion of Habermas's 'foundationalism' misses the point: Habermas's central contribution is not his provision of a theory of justification, although this is a significant contribution, but his understanding of the importance of communication to social relationships and the exploration and formation of cultural values. The theory of justification provides the framework for communication, to be sure. Here again, however, the importance of that framework derives from the conviction that the communicative processes in which values are discovered and shared must be free of deception and coercion. Perhaps postmodern theory contains a challenge to this conviction, but if so then that challenge itself, for Habermas, must offer more than a mere denial that normative foundations for thought and action are necessary.

The significance of Habermas's insights into the nature and role of communication can be illuminated by examining some applications of his critical theory to specific practices and institutions. In the concluding chapter, three analyses of distorted communication are presented, which are noteworthy for the complexity of the institutions that they succeed in analyzing, as well as the extent to which they extend the range of possible applications of Habermas's analysis of distorted communication beyond what is envisioned in his own work. In at least one case, this project also entails some major rethinking of Habermas's analysis of distorted communication.

CHAPTER 7

Critical Applications of the Theory

Habermas's American reception has been strongly influenced by the critical responses first of the positivists and then of the postmodernists, often with the result that he is regarded as a holdover of the past (whether because he is seen as too much the "speculative" philosopher in the Hegelian tradition or as too tied to the rationalism and liberal values of the Enlightenment). These impressions are unfortunate, because Habermas offers the only available systematic analysis of the contradictions of the postindustrial welfare state. This analysis, which presents the problem of modernity not merely as a product of economic crisis tendencies, but also as a problem that arises from the disintegration of the cultural and valuative basis of collective choice, is a valuable and "updated" alternative to Marxian analyses.

Without question, further critical development of Habermas's social theory would be welcome. Of special interest, from an American perspective, would be constructive criticism for the purpose of adapting Habermas's work to the special theoretical issues raised by the cultural and racial diversity, commercialization, and tremendous inequality of a society such as the United States. Habermas's criticism of the welfare state as the colonizer of the lifeworld, it should be remembered, is directed at a society that, by our standards, is relatively homogeneous and very solicitous of its citizens. Noncitizen residents of West Germany (for example, the "guest workers" from Turkey and Yugoslavia), of course, are another story, and their role in the affluent German economy is not considered in the development of Habermas's theory, nor by his critics. Given the increasingly important role of "aliens" in today's developed societies, it is odd that a theorist of such broad range as Habermas should overlook the importance of the internationalization (and continued emiseration) of the labor market to both the contemporary economy and contemporary cultural change.

Although the response among American social and political theorists to the potential directions in which Habermas's theory might be developed and transformed, in the context of these and other issues, so far has been limited, there exist several attempts, a few of them substantial, to carry out such projects. Three of them will be the focus of this chapter: an analysis of the mass media in the United States, an analysis of the politics of need interpretation in the welfare system, and an analysis of the role of the production of social psychological knowledge in liberal capitalism. Habermas's theory of rationality also has appeared in the critical analyses of educational institutions and practices, local government, consumer magazines, and motion picture advertisements.[1] These contributions illustrate that a partnership of philosophical social theory and social science, like the traditional partnership of the *Sozialwissenschaften* in Germany, could provide an arena for ideas about the state of culture and politics in the United States that now have difficulty finding a forum.

The three "applications" of Habermas presented in this chapter serve as more than mere instances of the use of his analysis of the ways in which communication is distorted in postindustrial society. There are ambiguities and potential tensions in Habermas's theory that would need to be understood and resolved before it could ever be "applied" at all straightforwardly. Perhaps the principle source of ambiguity in Habermas's critical theory is his definition and use of the distinction between the system and the lifeworld. Critics of Habermas have pointed to tensions between his functionalism and his hermeneuticism, and between his Marxian view of natural science, technology, and organizational rationality, on the one hand, and his Hegelian view of social theory on the other.[2] To some extent, these tensions can be dealt with simply by emphasizing the importance of the philosophical distinction that Habermas draws between functional and communicative rationality in making his puzzling distinction between the system and the lifeworld. However, some tensions and questions remain. There are at least two very important questions: the question of what has become of ideology critique in Habermas's recent theory, and the related question of the role of the analysis of class conflict in a critical theory of society. Because Habermas has shifted his focus away from ideology critique roughly since *The Theory of Communicative Action,* analyzing distortion of communication as functional rather than ideological, the status of the "producers of knowledge"—the information media, social policy analysts, and the sciences—has become unclear. One could ask, for example, what we should make of the increasing cooperation between industry and the natural and social sciences or of the commercialization of the information media. In a more general vein, one could ask whether Habermas's recent analysis of the colonization of the lifeworld and the crises it engenders captures all of the relevant ways in which communication is distorted in late capitalism. A related question is whether Habermas has not overlooked persisting class issues (tame though these may seem in West Germany itself) that continue to be objects of ideological obfuscation.

Each of the three projects presented in this chapter reintroduces either some form of critique of ideology, or an analysis of at least some of the aspects of a remaining class conflict, or both. However, each also addresses a specific institution, suggesting that the project is just as much an extension of Habermas's theory as a revision of it. The questions they raise and the general approaches they adopt are as follows. First, although the concept of communication is central to Habermas's theory, it is unclear where the mass media is supposed to fit in the scheme of the system and the lifeworld. Daniel Hallin engages in a history and straightforwardly Habermasian analysis of the role of the mass media in bringing about the end of public debate in the United States.[3] Second, how do the institutions of the welfare state in fact amount to a colonization of the lifeworld, as Habermas asserts they are? Nancy Fraser has employed Habermas's conceptual framework, though with fundamental modifications, to address the American welfare system and its interaction with its predominantly female clients-victims.[4] In yet a different vein again, what has become of Habermas's view of the production of non-Hegelian, 'positivist' social scientific and behavioral knowledge as a form of ideology (as it was presented in the years of *Knowledge and Human Interest*)? Philip Wexler has brought Habermas, Adorno and Horkheimer, and Marx together to construct a critical social psychology.[5] The following three sections give brief descriptions of these projects. In conclusion, we shall consider their significance as challenges to and extensions of Habermas's conception of critical theory.

The End of Public Debate: The Mass Media

Daniel Hallin begins his analysis of the cultural and political role of the mass media in the United States with the premise that public debate has very nearly come to an end in this country. The premise stands in need of an explanation, however; and Hallin's intention is to provide one, making use of Habermas's concepts of distorted and undistorted communication. In outline, Hallin's argument is that, partly as a result of the "colonization" of the news media by commercial as well as political-administrative interests and partly by the coincidental influence of positivism on editors and schools of journalism, the mass media have come to "take technical knowledge as a model for the reporting of the news."[6] Rather than develop the terms of political debate—the consequences of social policy choices for the various interests, groups, and classes involved—news reporting tends to reduce social and political issues to technical problems, and then inquire later whether they have or have not been solved successfully. This reductive approach to issues on the part of the mass media, combined with its ability to convey the impression that the matter is closed, is essentially equivalent to the near elimination of communication in the public domain.

This has not occurred as a result of conspiracy, but neither has it arisen by chance. Hallin argues that the history of the evolution of the mass media in the United States is one of centralization, commercialization, and to a relatively small extent, conformity to administrative interests. Prior to the advent of the penny press in the 1830s, the newspaper had been a forum of public debate between individuals and between political parties. The commercialization of the newspaper, made possible by advances in the technology of the press, brought with it dependence on advertising for revenue. Advertisers, in turn, sought a readership that crossed party lines, and communicated their desire for nonpartisan news coverage with their patronage. "Objective" journalism really began to emerge only in the 1920s, however, as positivism came into vogue among intellectuals. Between World War II and the 1960s, objective journalism assumed the extreme form of naive realism: the obligation to tell only the facts was taken to mean that journalism should refrain from interpretation. The Vietnam war, however, eventually spawned conflicting interpretations of the "facts." The White House "white papers" that journalists had relied on rather heavily, for example, conflicted with accounts from foreign correspondents and televised clips from the battlefield (note that Vietnam was the first—and, as of 1991, last—televised U.S. military engagement free of heavy censorship). To respond to this threat to their professionalism, journalists began to redirect the focus of public debate to technical issues, which could be discussed without raising any major political questions. "The whole of part II [of a December 1968 *CBS Evening News* report on "pacification" in Vietnam] was devoted to the computerized Hamlet Evaluation System (HES)," which produced the official figures on the progress of pacification. That was where Senator John Tunney came in; he was not there to discuss the wisdom or justice of U.S. policy in Vietnam but to offer an opposing view on the accuracy of the figures produced by the HES."[7] Because the discussion of ends is excluded from discourse with such a low level of political content, news reporting of this kind promotes only a "low level of collective will formation." Moreover, an additional message is communicated to the viewer-reader, contained in the performative rather than the propositional content, which implies that this level of will formation is all that there is to public debate. Hallin suggests that the authoritative and detached style in which news is reported conveys to the viewer reader the impression that the matter under discusssion is closed. Unlike genuine political discourse, in which the "I-You" relationship is established by raising validity claims, news reporting tends to treat the viewer-reader as an anonymous third-person observer rather than a participant in discourse.[8]

However, Hallin argues, the mass media cannot be absorbed by political interests to become the purveyors of a purely one-dimensional consciousness, as the Frankfurt School had suggested. Here Hallin alludes to Habermas's analysis of the legitimation crisis of the state. It might be suggested that the mass media have taken over the role of legitimating the state, from declining traditional associations. However, as Hallin argues, the mass media industry has its own legitimation needs, which do not always coincide with those of the state. Furthermore, as a for-profit industry, the mass media are due to be as anarchic as any participants in the marketplace. Most important, the state's needs for legitimacy cannot be met by ideology: such a maneuver would have to be unsuccessful, due to its incompatibility with the necessarily communicative nature of the formation of shared norms. Legitimation must issue from the rational acceptance of validity claims, and this acceptance cannot be imposed.

Hallin's analysis of the mass media, then, is not directly intended to revive the critique of ideology, but instead to draw attention to, and explain, the end of public debate in the United States. As it is described by Hallin, political discourse has been extensively "colonized," over the course of almost 200 years, by the functional rationality of the marketplace (though not as a legitimator of, but as a participant in, the marketplace). However, it could be argued that ideological consequences have followed from this colonization. Perhaps partisanship on the part of the mass media has not ended, but moved to an undefined center. Such a move might have hindered the definition of distinct party positions, which depend after all on the possibility of distinct interpretations of social and political affairs. It is also possible that the vacuum left by the end of mass participation in substantive political discourse leaves the members of our society vulnerable to simplistic and otherwise deceptive (ideological) interpretations of "current events." In short, Hallin's analysis points to the possibility that there are indirect ways in which ideology is produced with the cooperation of the mass media, and that the mass media prepare the ground for the acceptance of ideological positions that would not be accepted if collective will formation were not kept at such a low level.

Most important, however, Hallin's article illustrates Habermas's concern, not that particular hidden ideological agendas be revealed from a "universal" perspective, but that the culturally embodied critique of ideology and values which occurs in a strong public domain be restored. False consciousness is less of a danger than loss of consciousness. And as Hallin points out, the root of the danger lies in the fact that an increasing portion of the sources of public discourse are products on a mass market, rather than *communicative actions.*

The Politics of Need Interpretation and the Welfare System

The last three chapters of Nancy Fraser's *Unruly Practices* introduce the concept of the "politics of need interpretation" and employ that concept in an analysis of the American welfare system. The concept of need interpretation is familiar from Habermas's theory of justification for ethical norms (Chapter 4). In the discussion of normative validity claims, Habermas proposes that those needs and interests on the basis of which ethical and social norms are found to be valid or invalid are discovered collectively, by means of reflectively interpreting the significance of prereflective needs and interests. Fraser adds a new dimension to the discussion of need interpretation: that of gender. With the addition of this dimension, it becomes clear that American society sustains certain patterns of need interpretation, which become institutionalized, whereas others are suppressed. Thus, the needs of women (and other underprivileged classes or groups) are not interpreted in a univocal manner between the discourse of male-dominated institutions and the discourse of the women who so often find themselves in a dependent position with respect to them: there is a politics of need interpretation.

A relatively simple example of conflicting need interpretations is provided by the case of an adolescent mother receiving Aid to Families with Dependent Children (AFDC) who needs to support herself and her family but cannot afford job training or child care. (It should be noted that most AFDC recipients are women.) She may interpret her own needs as being for job training that will enable her to earn a sufficient living and for day care until she is able to complete job training. It is likely that the official interpretation of her needs by the administration of AFDC, however, identifies them as needs for motivation and emotional growth (to be provided by a psychiatric social worker) and for the means of subsistence for herself and her family, until she is sufficiently mature to take care of herself. This kind of conflict of need interpretations is weighted in favor of the welfare administration, largely because the administration's assumptions about the nature of women's work are solidly entrenched in the wider society as well. As a result, AFDC tends, counterproductively, to succeed principally in strapping its "clients" into their dependent positions.

The welfare system's interpretation of women's needs is distorted in part by its own requirement that those needs be "translated" into the standardized, quantifiable form that can be dealt with by the administration. But two additional features of the system contribute further distortion. First, a legal distinction is made between the recipients of unemployment and Social Security benefits (largely male), who are treated as bearers of rights to those benefits, and recipients of AFDC and other benefits aimed at "dysfunctional" families, who are guaranteed fewer rights with regard to their benefits. Second, the welfare recipient is treated as a deviant in need of therapy. By these means, the welfare system, which Fraser calls a "juridical-administrative-therapeutic state apparatus" (JAT), effectively suppresses the communicative politics of need interpretation:

> The JAT treats the interpretation of people's needs as pregiven and unproblematic, while itself redefining them as amenable to system-conforming satisfactions. Thus, the JAT shifts attention away from the question: Who interprets social needs and how? It tends to substitute the *juridical, administrative and therapeutic management of need satisfaction* for the *politics of need interpretation.* That is, it tends to substitute *monological, administrative processes of need definition* for *dialogical, participatory processes of need interpretation.*[9]

Thus far, Fraser's analysis of the dysfunctional effects of the welfare state, which, in this analysis, emerge in the lifeworld in the form of distorted need interpretation, could be seen as a more or less a direct extension of Habermas's analysis of the colonization of the lifeworld. However, Fraser points to the existence of a domain of contestation concerning the interpretation of needs. This domain, which she calls *the social,* exists in virtue of the fact that the JAT has ideological effects—its interpretation of its "clients'" needs—that directly conflict with the actual or potential interpretations by the welfare dependents of their own needs.[10] Thus the social is a potential arena for the critique of the ideology generated by the "experts" who represent the system and the system's mode of operation. Fraser locates in it such oppositional movements as feminism, lesbian and gay activism, and minority activism, along with the "experts," and conservative movements seeking to return the voices that raise "problematic" needs to their earlier private and marginal confines. By her analysis, then, the dysfunction of the American welfare system is not merely the result of its general tendency to interrupt the communicative processes of the lifeworld, but, more specifically, of the way in which it manages need satisfaction on the basis of a distorted interpretation of needs. That distorted interpretation has its roots both in prejudices about women and the poor and in the tendency of the mode of operation of the economic-administrative system to suppress the participation of women and minorities in need interpretation.

To counteract these distortions, Fraser suggests, the contestants must develop a *means of interpretation and communication* consonant with their own experience. Alternative need interpretations can emerge only with the emergence of narratives, vocabularies, and paradigms of argumentation that do not identify the needs of members of disenfranchised classes and groups as inherently illegitimate. The development of alternative means of interpretation and communication, such as that of feminism, is a form of cultural activism as well as a response to unjust treatment of "basic" needs. As such it is heterogeneous, because it recognizes the potential plurality of need interpretation, and challenges the assumption that there is a universal class of "basic" needs.

However, unlike the similar, though less well-developed, role that Habermas has envisioned for alternative cultures, Fraser's domain of the social crosses the public-private boundary, a boundary that Habermas leaves relatively undisputed. As a domain of contestation, the social allows for public conflicts that those in power would just as soon have remain private or otherwise inaudible. Therefore, Fraser argues, the distinction between the public and the private is itself a contestable issue. As it presently stands, the public-private distinction is drawn in a way that suppresses feminist need interpretation and contributes to the oppression of women. Women's unpaid domestic labor, for example, is relegated to the private domestic sphere, and the public discussion of such issues as domestic violence has been considered unseemly.

Fraser's concept of the social comes close to Habermas's ideal of public discourse, though Fraser emphasizes the need for critique that is not largely confined to the lifeworld, but that engages in ongoing confrontation with the ways in which specific features of the lifeworld and the system interact to maintain gender and class domination. An approach that sees the lifeworld and the system not as uncoupled, but as interactive, is especially important, in her view, for a feminist critical theory.[11] Her analysis of the circumstances of women clients of the welfare state offers a valuable example of how such a critical theory might be developed.

Social Psychology as Social Ignorance: A Critical Approach to Social Psychology

Philip Wexler's book *Critical Social Psychology* makes the argument that social psychology produces social ignorance. Although the argument employs the critical theory of the Frankfurt School, it is consonant with, and in part draws from, Habermas's views during the early 1970s on the potential ideological role of positivist science.[12] (Wexler's book was published before the publication of *The Theory of Communicative Action,* and he cites only two of Habermas's earlier publications: *Legitimation Crisis* [1975], and *Toward a Rational Society* [1970]). In particular, Wexler employs Habermas's insistence, against Marx, that social science need not be ideological, but that only a critical social science can hope to be nonideological. *Critical Social Psychology,* then, is an analysis from a critical theoretical perspective of social psychology as it is now practiced and as it could be practiced were it to become a critical social psychology.

The discussion of Habermas's response to positivism in the first part of Chapter 6 showed that, for Habermas, social science becomes ideological when it reduces all rational action to instrumentally rational action, thereby precluding the possibility of critical reflection on the communicative processes in which ends are discovered, articulated, and chosen. Social science is ideology because it inhibits critique. Wexler combines this analysis of 'positivist' social science as ideology with an analysis, derived from Adorno and Horkheimer, of *cultural* domination. For Wexler, social science does not merely inhibit critique, but produces social ignorance by misleadingly reconceptualizing the contradictions of social and economic life under liberal capitalism: "High culture, mass culture, and scientific culture all now include as constitutive ideological processes: compartmentalizing sublimation, repetitive repression, and silent denial. If social psychology now functions as a legitimating, selective reprocessor and packager of the methods of cultural contradiction containment, it does so through exactly such patterned and identifiable modes of constructed cultural domination."[13]

The "cultural contradiction containment" of which Wexler speaks is a defense against collective self-understanding, social knowledge, and the potential use of this knowledge for social and self-realization.[14] This "containment" is a form of cultural domination, the methods of which are themselves cultural in nature. According to Adorno and Horkheimer, for example, mass culture promises entertainment, rather than self-realization, both displacing and deceptively redefining unmet needs.[15] That one in fact is not able to make significant choices about how one will live is masked by the variety of choices among different commodities. Wexler's argument is that social psychology's role always has been to disguise and legitimate the methods of cultural domination. Originally, social psychology was called on to legitimate and "repackage" the methods of socialization devised for reconciling the laissez-faire individualism promoted by capitalism with the increasing need for effective cooperation among the members and employees of private corporations. The first task of social psychology was to construct the new, oxymoronic notion of a "socialized individual." "Cooperation and adjustment were heralded as necessary to social progress, and if the corporate liberal theorists of the Progressive era were later to try to construct institutionally—through educational reform—a social method for the production of cooperative individual adjustment to collective need, the social psychologists constructed the theoretical foundation for the social compromises of the Progressive period."[16]

Later, during World War II, the aims of psychological warfare and the organizational demands of a heightened industrial production transformed social psychology into a force of production. More recently, Wexler argues, the increasing commercialization of everyday life has demanded correspondingly more regulation of "everyday" interaction. The task of social psychology is now, even more than ever, to keep people ignorant of the ways in which social relations are shaped.[17] Social psychology does not accomplish this task alone, of course. Rather, it assists and reinforces popular methods of "social ignorance production." Given that, for example, the level of discourse generally is low in the mass media, the fact that social psychologists study, say, "conformity and obedience" among the individual participants of the Watergate scandal, excluding any analysis of the institutions within which these individuals acted, the social psychological studies contribute to keeping the understanding of this and similar issues at a low level. Other examples of the reinforcement of cultural reifications by social psychology is found in its approaches to the study of aggression, self-esteem, and solidarity:

> The situational reframing of social interdependence issues and questions of social fragmentation are experimentally explored as socially influenced matters of individual choice. In studies of aggression and violence, national and international questions soon become—by the mediating redefinition of social determination as learning—studies of the effects of television programs. . . . Similarly, questions of solidarity are discussed as problems in the study of interpersonal attraction. Social solidarity becomes liking, which, in turn, becomes attractiveness, which is then largely putatively determined by physical appearance and trait similarity. Self-worth is in no way related to invidious social stratification.[18]

A critical social psychology, as Wexler describes it, includes three dimensions: a Marxian theory of the social relations of capitalism, an identification of the contradictions inherent in cultural reifications, and a class analysis of social psychology itself. Wexler argues that alienation, commodity fetishism, and exploitation are forms of social interaction—if understood only as economic processes, they are understood too narrowly. This Marxian analysis of social relations then is employed to reveal the contradictions underlying social psychological theory, and specifically, its theories of "interaction," "self," and "intimacy." All three of these latter phenomena, according to Wexler, in fact are disappearing, due to a social matrix that refuses and precludes them, while appearing to offer them as possibilities. Social psychology clouds the processes by which an "instrumentalized" social existence has evolved—an existence that is becoming incompatible with interaction, self and intimacy—essentially by emptying these concepts of their content.[19]

There are some rough parallels here to the shape that critical sociology has recently taken for Habermas, who combines a functional analysis of the relations of production with a hermeneutic analysis of culture. Wexler's use of Frankfurt School critical theory is the means by which he reintroduces psychological and ***kulturkritisch*** (culture-critical) dimensions into Marxian analysis, which, in his view, lately has tended to become a branch of positivist economics.[20] However, two obvious divergences between Wexler and the recent Habermas stand out: Wexler's critical social psychology is (1) the critique of an ideology (conventional social psychology) that (2) has its origins in class conflict.

Concluding Remarks

The previous three sections should have shown that there is greater potential significance to the critical theory of Jürgen Habermas than has been realized thus far. At the same time, they recognize respects in which some important issues have been inadequately worked out in Habermas's work. As mentioned at the beginning of this chapter, the issues raised by sympathetic and critical readers alike often raise the questions of class conflict and ideology in one way or another. Whether these inadequacies represent flaws in Habermas's analytic categories or method is less than clear.

In his 1986 article, "The New Obscurity: The Crisis of the Welfare State and the Exhaustion of Utopian Energies," Habermas assembles part of a response to these questions, out of his views about the loss of revolutionary momentum and utopian thinking in the late capitalist welfare state.[21] Taking as a given that the discourse of utopia has come to an end, Habermas explains its demise as part of the end of the "laboring society"—the end, in other words, of the Marxist vision of the overcoming of alienated labor, the end of the prominent role of labor in the economy, and now, the threat to the social democratic vision of a prosperous compromise between capitalism and labor in the welfare state. The utopian contents of Western social democracies (of whom the United States might be called a borderline member) largely had been drawn from that of the laboring society: Marx's society of collective owners of the means of production. But the class conflict that enraged Marx has been transformed, and the utopian society of the early socialists has lost credibility as a result. Coming to an end as well is the critique of ideology, which had the revelation of a new society as its aim and inspiration.

Needless to say, this analysis is not entirely satisfactory from the perspective of the Western Hemisphere, whether viewed at the level of the city, country, or continent; nor, of course, is it satisfactory from a global perspective. Ideological accounts of regional conflicts abound, and the involvement of class in these conflicts is impossible to miss: Marxian theory thus is alive, though not well, in this hemisphere for a reason.

At the same time it is clear that there is little energy for utopia here in the United States at the end of the twentieth century, as elsewhere among the Western democracies. The three authors just presented concur in this and wish, with Habermas, to point us generally in the direction of a revival of public debate. Nancy Fraser finds one already in existence, though it avoids being properly "public" in Habermas's sense. Her inclusion of a Foucaultian angle on the origins of "needs talk" may have contributed to her identification of the social as a domain of inevitable contestation rather than of rationally motivated consensus.[22] Habermas, however, frankly expresses some concern about the possible sources of new utopian contents: "The formation of political will must now draw from that same wellspring [solidarity]; it should seek to influence the boundaries and the interchange between communicatively structured areas of life, on the one hand, and the state and the economy, on the other."[23] The appeal to the wellspring of solidarity may convey some sense of paradox, given that the communal prerequisites of solidarity themselves are eroding, by Habermas's own account. On the other hand, it is clear to Habermas that two illusions are gone: that of the utopian potential of the laboring society, and that of the utopia as a "concrete totality of future possibilities." The utopian potential found in the laboring society, in Habermas's view, now can be derived only from the "communication community." However, it would be a mistake to suppose that formal notion of the ideal speech situation imposes any particular "concrete form of life," understood as a totality. Whatever new utopian contents evolve, they will not have the totalitarian structure of a society based on instrumental or functional reason. They must be values identified in free communication.

The concern has been expressed, especially with regard to Habermas's discourse ethics, that his theory has abandoned the utopian dimension of traditional critical theory. Joel Whitebook expresses this concern well;

> Can we preclude the possibility of a meaningless emancipation? In complex societies, emancipation means the participatory transformation of administrative decision structures. Is it possible that one day an emancipated human race could encounter itself within an expanded space of discursive formation of will and yet be robbed of the light in which it is capable of interpreting its life as something good? The revenge of a culture exploited over millenia for the legitimation of domination would then take this form: right at the moment of overcoming age-old repression, it would harbor no violence but it would have no content either.[24]

Because his theory of communicative rationality does not offer more than the formal conditions for a living culture, which must define its own conception of the good life on the basis of its own experience, Habermas's theory is not a utopian theory. His concept of aesthetic-cultural reason can count as little more than the "placeholder" of the good life. But would we have it any other way? Culture, no matter how large a geographical area it comes to occupy, must always be local. A consequence of Habermas's warning is that with the increasing functionalization and ensuing standardization of the lifeworld, our ability to belong or be embedded in a particular community with a strong identity, whether a rural *pays* or an urban "crowd," whether an ethnic Finnish logging village in Oregon or an ironist clique of intellectuals in Virginia, is weakened. Culture is coming less and less naturally; more and more we rely on the canned version.

Notes

Introduction

1. McCarthy, Thomas, *The Critical Theory of Jurgen Habermas* (Cambridge, Mass.: MIT Press, 1978); David Held, *Introduction to Critical Theory: Horkheimer to Habermas* (Berkeley: University of California Press, 1980); John B. Thompson and David Held, Eds., *Habermas: Critical Debates* (Cambridge, Mass.: MIT Press, 1982); Richard Bernstein, Ed. *Habermas and Modernity,* (Cambridge, Mass.: MIT Press, 1985); Martin Jay, *Marxism and Totality: The Adventures of a Concept from Lukacs to Habermas* (Berkeley: University of California Press, 1984)

2. Studies in Contemporary German Social Thought, Thomas McCarthy, general editor (Cambridge, Mass.: MIT Press). The series includes Claus Offe's *Contradictions of the Welfare State* (1984), Hans Blumenberg's *The Legitimacy of the Modern Age* (1983), and Hans Georg Gadamer's *Reason in the Age of Science* (1982). Gadamer and Offe have contributed significantly to Habermas.

3. Ingram, David, *Habermas and the Dialectic of Reason* (New Haven, Conn.: Yale University Press, 1987); Rick Roderick, *Habermas and the Foundations of Critical Theory* (New York: St. Martin's Press, 1986); Seyla Benhabib, *Critique, Norm, and Utopia* (New York: Columbia University Press, 1986); Stephen White, *The Recent Work of Jürgen Habermas* (New York: Cambridge University Press, 1988); Tom Rockmore, *Habermas on Historical Materialism* (Indianapolis: Indiana University Press, 1989).

4. The citation is from Habermas's *Theory and Practice,* trans. John Viertel (Boston: Beacon Press, 1973), p. 212.

5. See especially Seyla Benhabib, *Critique, Norm, and Utopia;*

Martin Jay, *Marxism and Totality;* David Held, *Introduction to Critical Theory.*

6. Habermas finds this assessment first in Hegel. See pp. 156ff, in Chapter 6 of this book, concerning the 'problem of modernity'. Contemporary 'neoconservative' critics of modernity include Daniel Bell (e.g., Bell,1976) and Arnold Gehlen (e.g., Gehlen,1940).

7. This problem is first developed in Max Weber (1904–1905), as what Habermas calls the "thesis of a loss of freedom." In English, *The Protestant Ethic and the Spirit of Capitalism* (New York: Charles Scribner's Sons, 1958). See pp. 181–182.

8. Habermas adopted this hypothesis from early twentieth century anthropology. See *TCA* I, 43–53.

9. Raymond Geuss, *The Idea of a Critical Theory* (Cambridge: Cambridge University Press, 1981)

10. See, for example, *TCA* II, p. 196: "The modern form of understanding is too transparent to provide a niche for this structural violence by means of inconspicuous restrictions on communication." For a well-supported challenge to this view, see James Bohman, "Formal Pragmatics and Social Criticism," *Philosophy and Social Criticism* 11, 4 (Fall 1986): 331–353.

1. An Outline of Habermas's Critical Theory

1. The distinction between therapeutic and diagnostic critiques is my own; not Habermas's. I find it useful because it is a familiar distinction, and it does not distort Habermas's intent.

2. In the view of some, this weakens the critical potential of Habermas's theory, because it forces a distinction between critical theory and "culture-critical" reflection on the good life. Related objections are discussed in Chapters 3 and 4.

3. This characterization derives from Marx, "Letter to A. Ruge, September 1843," in *Karl Marx: Early Writings,* ed. L. Colletti, trans. Rodney Livingstone and Gregor Benton (New York: McGraw Hill, 1975) p. 209. I am indebted to Nancy Fraser's book *Unruly Practices* (Minneapolis: University of Minnesota Press, 1989) for the recognition of the significance of this passage.

4. See note 7 in the Introduction.

5. Zoltan Tar, *The Frankfurt School* (New York: Schocken Books, 1985), p. xiii. Cf. Max Horkheimer and Theodor Adorno: "The dilemma that faced us in our work proved to be the first phenomenon for investigation: the self-destruction of the Enlightenment." From *Dialectic of Enlightenment* (New York: Continuum, 1982), p. xiii.

6. Marcuse, and to some extent Horkheimer, diverged from this pessimistic view of reason. See Herbert Marcuse, "Industrialization and Capitalism in the Work of Max Weber," in *Negations: Essays in Critical Theory,* with translations from the German by Jeremy Shapiro (London: Free Association Books, 1988).

7. "What Is Universal Pragmatics?" in *CES,* pp. 28ff. There is a fourth validity claim, the intelligibility claim, but this applies to correct usage of the language only and does not require rational consensus for its vindication. See *CES,* p. 64.

8. This thought is developed, for example, in the essay, "Historical Materialism and the Development of Normative Structures" in *CES.* It is also inherent in Habermas's conviction that illocutionary force is what enables the speaker to establish a relationship with the hearer. See *CES,* 34–35.

9. See Seyla Benhabib, *Critique, Norm, and Utopia,* and Thomas McCarthy, "Reflections on Rationalization" in *Habermas and Modernity,* ed. Richard Bernstein (Cambridge, Mass.: MIT Press, 1985), pp. 176–191, especially 184–186.

10. *TCA* I, 6–7; see also, McCarthy's Introduction, p. xii.

2. A Consensus Theory of Truth and Knowledge

1. The consensus theory of truth is first defended in Habermas's 1972 paper, "Wahrheitstheorien," which appears in *Vorstudien und Erganzungen zur Theorie des kommunikativen Handelns* (Frankfurt am Main: Suhrkamp Verlag, 1984), pp. 555ff. This rather technical article provoked a number of criticisms, some of which were addressed in "A Reply to my Critics," in J. B. Thompson, and D. Held, Eds., *Habermas—Critical Debates* (Cambridge, Mass: MIT Press, 1982), pp. 219–283. The theory of truth is defended again in *The Theory of Communicative Action,* with more attention to its role in the explanation of action than to technical issues.

2. Such as, for example, the theories of meaning proposed by

Michael Dummett ("What Is a Theory of Meaning?" in Samuel Guttenplan, Ed., *Mind and Language* (Oxford: Clarendon Press, 1975); and Donald Davidson, *Inquiries into Truth and Interpretation* (New York: Oxford University Press, 1984).

3. This is a strong premise, which needs argument. Habermas's defense of this claim is discussed in Chapter 4.

4. Susan Haack, "Theories of Truth," in *Philosophy of Logics* (Cambridge: Cambridge University Press, 1978), pp. 87–134. The two latter types of theories of truth—semantic (e.g., Alfred Tarski) and redundancy (Frank Ramsey)—are explicitly formulated to avoid making epistemological claims and "cut across" the first three types (p. 88).

5. Cf. Habermas: "Die Idee der Wahrheit lässt sich nur mit Bezugnahme auf die diskursive Einlösung von Geltungsansprüchen entfalten. . . . Der Sinn von Wahrheit, der in der Pragmatik von Behauptungen impliziert ist, lässt sich erst hinreichend klären, wenn wir angeben können, was 'diskursive Einlösung' von erfahrunsfundierten Geltungsansprüchen bedeutet. Genau dies ist das Ziel einer Konsensustheorie der Wahrheit." From "Wahrheitstheorien," *V,* 135–136.

6. See note 4.

7. The same point applies to the other validity claims. See Habermas's discussion of Weber's theory of action in *TCA* I, 279–286, which examines the *purpose* of validity claims.

8. For example, Alfred Tarski, "The Concept of Truth in Formalized Languages" [1935]; reprinted in A. Tarski, *Logic, Semantics, Metamathematics,* ed. John Corcoran, 2d ed. (Indianapolis: Hackett Publishing Co., 1983).

9. M. Dummett, Preface, in *Truth and Other Enigmas* (Cambridge, Mass.: Harvard University Press, 1978), p. xxi.

10. Habermas's lo c of discourse is largely derived from Stephen Toulmin's *The Uses of rgument* (Cambridge: Cambridge University Press, 1964).

11. Such as Donald Davidson, for example, in, "A Coherence Theory of Truth and Knowledge," in *Truth and Interpretation: Perspectives on the Philosophy of Donald Davidson,* ed. Ernest Lepore (Oxford: Basil Blackwell, Ltd., 1986), pp. 307–319.

12. See Habermas, "A Reply to My Critics," p. 277.

3. *A Consensus Theory of Normative Validity*

1. J. Habermas, "Discourse Ethics—Notes Towards a Groundwork" ("Diskursethik: Notizen zu einem Begründungsprogramm"), in *Moral Consciousness and Communicative Action* (Cambridge, Mass.: MIT Press, 1990), p. 43. First printed in *Moralbewusstsein und kommunikatives Handeln* (Frankfurt am Main: Suhrkamp Verlag, 1983). For a statement of this "familiar conviction," see, for example, A. MacIntyre, *After Virtue* (Notre Dame, Ind.: University of Notre Dame Press, 1981), p. 52.

2. In ibid. Noncognitivism is a category of positions in ethics, which includes a broad variety of positions all of which hold that value judgments cannot be justified or proven in the same way as statements of fact or logic.

3. R. M. Hare, *The Language of Morals* (Oxford: Clarendon Press, 1952), p. 69: "Thus a complete justification of a decision would consist of a complete account of its effects, together with a complete account of the principles which it observed, and the effects of observing those principles for, of course, it is the effects (what obeying them actually consists in) which give content to the principles too. Thus, if pressed to justify a decision completely, we have to give a complete specification of the *way of life* of which it is a part."

4. See, for example, "The Scientization of Politics and Public Opinion," in *Toward a Rational Society* (Boston: Beacon Press, 1970), p. 66.

5. See Hare, *The Language of Morals;* and Habermas, *MCCA,* p. 44.

6. Hare, ibid., 68–69.

7. J. Habermas, "Wahrheitstheorien," in *V,* p. 165; *MCCA,* p. 65.

8. J. Habermas, "A Postscript to *Knowledge and Human Interests,*" *Philosophy of the Social Sciences* 3 (1973): 177.

9. Habermas, *V,* p. 139: "Wahrhaftigkeitsansprüche können nur in Handlunszusammenhängen engelöst werden"; and *CES,* p. 64: "the truthfulness of [an] utterance can only be checked against the consistency of his subsequent behavior." But see *TCA* I, 334.

10. The distinction between the just or ethical life, governed by universal norms, and the good or happy life, governed by reflection on the totality of values present to the subject, reflects the Hegelian division between "morality" (the moral law) and "Sittlichkeit" (the ethical life). Hegel argued that Kant's ethical theory failed to account for that

aspect of moral consciousness which is concerned with the good life. Seyla Benhabib suggests that a "cognitivist bias" still is present in Habermas's discourse ethics. See *Critique, Norm, and Utopia* (New York: Columbia University Press, 1986), pp. 317ff., and pp. 46ff. below.

11. Social-cultural "experimentation," for Habermas, is linked to the pressures put on culture by the functional rationalization of society. Apparently for this reason he often speaks of "new social movements" as various forms of protest against bureaucatization, rather than directly engaging them as political movements or forms of ethical criticism. See *TCA,* pp. 395–396; *Observations on the Spiritual Situation of the Age,* pp. 27–28.

12. For example, by Seyla Benhabib. See pp. 46ff. below.

13. Habermas, *MCCA,* p. 104.

14. Nancy Fraser's work on the politics of need interpretation can be seen as a development of this possibility, though one that is at the same time moderately critical of Habermas. See Chapter 7 of this book, and Fraser, *Unruly Practices* (Minneapolis: University of Minnesota Press, 1989), pp. 144–187.

15. Immanuel Kant, *Foundations of the Metaphysics of Morals,* Lewis White Beck (Chicago: University of Chicago Press, 1950).

16. A similar, though far more extensively developed criticism is made by Benhabib in *Critique, Norm, and Utopia* pp. 316–327. Benhabib links this problem to the more general issue of how adherence to highly abstract principles possibly can be motivated. This issue was first raised by Hegel as an objection to Kant.

17. Rawls argues that a suitably defined hypothetical position, called the *original position,* can be used to determine the basic principles of justice. See John Rawls, *A Theory of Justice* (Cambridge, Mass.: Harvard University Press, 1972), pp. 118–182.

18. S. Lukes, "Of Gods and Demons: Habermas and Practical Reason," in *Habermas: Critical Debates,* ed. J. Thompson and D. Held (London: Macmillan Press, 1982), p. 145.

19. See especially Karl-Otto Apel, "Das Apriori der Kommunikationsgesellschaft," in Apel, Ed., *Transformation der Philosophie* (Frankfurt am Main: Suhrkamp Verlag, 1973); and "Das Problem der philosophischen Letztbegründung im Lichte einer transzendentalen Sprachpragmatik," in B. Kanitschneider, Ed., *Sprache und Erkenntnis* (Innsbruck: 1976).

20. See note 1.

21. See Apel, 1973, p. 55f.

22. See, for example, G. E. Moore, "True and False Beliefs," *Some Main Problems of Philosophy* (London: Macmillan, 1953), pp. 270–287.

23. Habermas borrows all pragmatic rules mentioned in "Discourse Ethics" from R. Alexy, "Eine Theorie des Praktischen Diskurses," in W. Ölmüller, Ed., *Normenbegründung, normendurchsetzung* (Paderborn: 1978). Alexy worked out a system of rules for Habermasian practical discourse.

24. Albrecht Wellmer, *Ethik und Dialog* (Frankfurt am Main: Suhrkamp Verlag, 1986), especially pp. 102–113; Benhabib, *Critique, Norm, and Utopia,* especially pp. 297–327.

25. Wellmer, ibid., p. 108.

26. Benhabib, *Critique, Norm, and Utopia* pp. 306–307.

27. J. Habermas, "Morality and Ethical Life: Does Hegel's Critique of Kant Apply to Discourse Ethics?" in *MCCA,* pp. 195–215.; originally printed as "Moralität und Sittlichkeit: Treffen Hegels Einwände gegen Kant auch auf die Diskursethik zu?" *Revue Internationale de Philosophie* 42, no 166 (1988): 320–337.

28. Ibid., p. 204 (*MCCA*).

29. See *LC,* pp. 97–102.

4. The Theory of Communicative Competence

1. J. Habermas, in Richard Bernstein, Ed., *Habermas and Modernity* (Cambridge, Mass.: MIT Press, 1985), p. 209.

2. Habermas's principal recent discussions of aesthetic reason occur in *PDM,* especially pp. 45–50 (in addition, the discussions of postmodernism and Adorno address what Habermas sees as an "aestheticizing" tendency in recent continental philosophy); "Modernity Versus Postmodernity," *New German Critique* 22, (1981): 3–14; "Questions and Counterquestions," in Bernstein, *Habermas and Modernity,* pp. 192–216, especially pp. 199–203; and "Modern and Post-Modern Architecture," in Habermas, *The New Conservatism,* ed. and trans. Shierry Weber Nicholson (Cambridge, Mass.: MIT Press, 1989). "Architecture" specifically discusses the relation to functionalism of modern and postmodern architecture. See also *TCA* I, p. 334.

3. Habermas, in Bernstein, *Habermas and Modernity,* p. 203.

4. *See, for example, Nancy Fraser's "Women, Welfare and the Politics of Need Interpretation"* Hypatia 2, no. 1 (1987): 103–121, for an application of the idea of need interpretation in addressing problems within our welfare system, an arena quite removed from art criticism. This article is reprinted in Fraser, *Unruly Practices* (Minneapolis: University of Minnesota Press, 1989).

6. David Ingram, *Habermas and the Dialectic of Reason* (New Haven, Conn.: Yale University Press, 1987), pp. 179–186. Ingram refers to Habermas's tentative acceptance of a suggestion from Albrecht Wellmer in "Questions and Counterquestions" in Bernstein, *Habermas and Modernity;* see especially pp. 202–203.

7. Ingram, ibid., p. 186.

8. Ingram, ibid.

9. Ibid., see especially pp. 180–186. Ingram refers to Habermas's "Questions and Counterquestions," p. 203.

10. This is Seyla Benhabib's principal criticism of Habermas's work, in *Critique, Norm, and Utopia* (New York: Columbia University Press, 1986).

11. Habermas, "Questions and Counterquestions," p. 203.

12. See Habermas, "What is Universal Pragmatics?" in *Communication and the Evolution of Society* (Boston: Beacon Press, 1979); originally published in German in 1976.

13. The ideal of rational consensus is anticipated, even though it cannot be actualized, in communicative action. The achievement of "mutual understanding" in a loose sense, which can include a respectful and rationally motivated dissension, in contrast, is actualizable. Though the ideal of the rational consensus continues to be operative as an "anticipated ideal" in Habermas's views, this should not be taken to mean that we must achieve consensus in all or even most of our affairs. See *TCA* I, 307.

14. See Noam Chomsky, *Aspects of the Theory of Syntax* (Cambridge, Mass.: MIT Press, 1965)

15. Gilbert Ryle, "Knowing How and Knowing That," *Proceedings of the Aristotelian Society* 46 (1946).

16. The construction of a universal pragmatic model of linguistic usage follows a procedure of rational reconstruction of a pretheoretical

competence, which Habermas calls a *maeutic method.* A *maeutic method* is a method for making implicit knowledge explicit "through the choice of suitable examples and counterexamples, through contrast and similarity relations, through translation, paraphrase, and so on" (Habermas, *CES* p. 19)

17. H. P. Grice, "Logic and conversation," in P. Cole and J. L. Morgan, Eds., *Syntax and Semantics 3: Speech Acts* (New York: Academic Press, 1975), pp. 41–58; and "Further Notes on Logic and Conversation," in P. Cole, Ed., *Syntax and Semantics 9: Pragmatics* (New York: Academic Press, 1978), pp. 113–128.

18. J. Habermas, "Towards a Theory of Communicative Competence," *Inquiry* 13, no. 4, (1970): 373.

19. Habermas's argument for this claim is found in *TCA,* I, pp. 311ff.

20. Thomas McCarthy has argued that Habermas's classification of these relations is not altogether clear in "Reflections on Rationalization in *The Theory of Communicative Action*" in *Habermas and Modernity,* pp. 176–191. As will become evident in Chapter 5, Habermas's "actor-world" relations also provide a framework for the analysis and reconstruction of the historical development of culture. In brief, these kinds of relations are spheres in which cultural development or rationalization takes place. Habermas believes that three possible actor-world relations, including the third-person attitude toward the social and subjective worlds, are not spheres of rationalization. As McCarthy points out, the motivations for this belief are not evident.

21. This argument begins on page 288 of *TCA* I.

22. See J. L. Austin, *How to Do Things With Words,* ed. J. O. Urmson and Marina Sbisa (Cambridge, Mass.: Harvard University Press, 1962), p. 118.

23. Ibid. To secure uptake is to succeed in bringing the hearer to correctly recognize the type of act one is performing. When the act itself succeeds, it "takes effect."

24. Erling Skjei develops an objection to this argument in "A Comment on Performative, Subject, and Proposition in Habermas's Theory of Communication," *Inquiry* 28: 87–105. See especially pp. 90–93. See also Habermas's reply in "Reply to Skjei," pp. 105–122.

25. Albrecht Welmer, *Ethik und Dialog* (Frankfurt am Main: Suhrkamp, 1986), pp. 201–208.

26. Ibid., p. 208, my translation.

27. The very paper to which Wellmer is responding in the preceding argument discusses identity formation in modern societies: "Konnen komplexe Gesellschaften eine vernünftige Identität ausbilden?" in J. Habermas and D. Henrich, *Zwei Reden Aus Aulass des Hegel-Preises* (Frankfurt am Main: Suhrkamp, 1974); and abridged English version: "On Social Identity," *Telos* (Spring 1974): 91–103.

5. The Critique of Societal Rationalization

1. Habermas's principal references are to Max Weber, *Economy and Society* (Berkeley, 1978), and "Religious Rejections of the World" in H. H. Gerth and C. Wright Mills, Eds., *From Max Weber* (New York: Oxford University Press, 1958); G. H. Mead, *Mind, Self and Society,* ed. C. Morris (Chicago: University of Chicago Press, 1962); Emile Durkheim, *The Division of Labor in Society* (New York: Free Press of Glencoe, 1933), *The Elementary Forms of Religious Life* (New York: Collier Books, 1965), and *Sociology and Philosophy* (New York: Free Press, 1974); Alfred Schutz, *The Structure of the Lifeworld,* ed. Thomas Luckmann (Evanston, Ill.: Northwestern University Press, 1973); and Talcott Parsons, *Action Theory and Human Condition* (New York, 1978) and *Social Systems and the Evolution of Action Theory* (New York, 1977).

2. This point is made in, for example, the following passage from *LC,* p. 11: "The extension of system autonomy is dependent on developments in the other two dimensions—the development of productive forces (truth) and the alteration of normative structures (correctness/appropriateness)." This argument will be discussed further later.

3. Alfred Schutz and Thomas Luckmann, *The Structures of the Lifeworld* (Evanston, Ill.: Northwestern University Press, 1973), p. 15.

4. Ibid., p. 3.

5. Max Weber, *The Protestant Ethic and the Spirit of Capitalism,* trans. Talcott Parsons (New York: Charles Scribner's Sons, 1958), p. 27. Weber acknowledges here that full support for his hypothesis would require comparative study with non-European cultures.

6. In Habermas's opinion, Weber failed to keep in mind the alternatives open to a society at a given time, thus failing to make clear whether he thought any modernizing society would *have* to progress by the same means through a Protestant ethic.

7. Here Habermas adopts George Herbert Mead's concept of a "generalized other." See *TCA* II, 35–37.

8. The general theory of action is a functionalist explanation of societal change that employs the "action frame of reference," or the assumption that it is necessary to take both the actor and the situation of action into account in sociological explanation. Its outlines were first formulated in Talcott Parsons, *The Structure of Social Action* (Glencoe, Ill.: The Free Press, 1949).

9. The distinction between social and system (functional) integration is drawn from David Lockwood, "Social Integration and System Integration," in G. K. Zollochan and W. Hirsch, Eds., *Explorations in Social Change* (London: Routledge and Kegan Paul, 1964), pp. 244–257.

10. *LC,* Part II; for a brief list, see pp. 49–50.

11. Ibid., pp. 81–84.

12. This point and the relationships between the four crisis tendencies are developed in Part II of *LC.*

13. Some of the essays by Claus Offe that are noted in *LC* appear in translation in Offe, *Contradictions of the Welfare State,* ed. John Keane (Cambridge, Mass.: MIT Press, 1984); or in Offe, *Disorganized Capitalism,* ed. John Keane (Cambridge, Mass.: MIT Press, 1985).

14. *LC,* pp. 55–57.

15. *TCA* II, p. 371.

16. See, for example, Gena Corea, *The Hidden Malpractice* (New York: Harper and Row, 1985).

17. Nancy Fraser, "What's Critical about Critical Theory? The Case of Habermas and Gender," *New German Critique* 35 (Spring–Summer 1985): 97–131. This essay appears in Fraser, *Unruly Practices* (Minneapolis: University of Minnesota Press, 1989).

18. Karl Marx, *Grundrisse der Kritik der Politischen Ökonomie* (Harmondsworth, Middlesex: Penguin Books, 1973), p. 257.

19. See *TCA,*. I, p. 346; David Held, *Introduction to Critical Theory* (Berkeley: University of California Press, 1980), pp. 65–70.

20. *TCA,* II, p. 334.

21. Ibid., p. 341.

22. James F. Bohman, "Formal Pragmatics and Social Criticism" *Philosophy and Social Criticism* 11, no. 4 (Fall 1986).

23. Daniel Hallin, "The American News Media: A Critical Theory Perspective," in *Critical Theory and Public Life,* ed. John Forester (Cambridge, Mass.: MIT Press, 1985).

24. Fraser, *Unruly Practices;* "Toward a Discourse Ethic of Solidarity," *Praxis International* 5, no. 4 (January 1986); "Women, Welfare and the Politics of Need Interpretation," *Hypatia* 2, no. 1 (Winter 1987). Both essays appear in *Unruly Practices.*

6. Two Challenges: Positivism and Postmodernism

1. Michael Lessnoff, "Technique, Critique and Social Science," in *Philosophical Disputes in the Social Sciences,* ed. S. C. Brown; David Papineau, *For Science in the Social Sciences* (New York: St. Martin's Press, 1978); Adolf Grunbaum, *The Foundations of Psychoanalysis: A Philosophical Critique* (Los Angeles: University of California Press,1984).

2. *Erkenntnis und Interesse* (1968; *Knowledge and Human Interest* [1971]) was the culmination of Habermas's development of a critique of neopositivism. Methodological dualism was first defended in *Zur Logik der Sozialwissenschaften* in 1967 (under another title; the English translation is entitled *On the Logic of the Social Sciences*). *Toward a Rational Society* (1970; German text 1968, 1969) includes several essays on scientism and technocracy.

3. For example, the essays in *Lectures on the Philosophical Discourse of Modernity* (Cambridge, Mass.: MIT Press, 1988), and in *Moral Consciousness and Communicative Action* (Cambridge, Mass.: MIT Press, 1990).

4. Thomas McCarthy, "The New Historicism" (unpublished manuscript, 1987).

5. Habermas defends methodological dualism in the course of his critical response to the claims of positivist philosophy of behavioral science in *On the Logic of the Social Sciences* (Cambridge, Mass.: MIT Press, 1988) and later in *TCA,* I, Chapter 1, Section 4.

6. This position derives from Max Weber, who defended it in the *Methodenstreit* [Dispute on Method] of the 1880s and 1890s.

7. Charles Taylor, *Philosophical Papers, Volume 2: Philosophy and the Human Sciences* (Cambridge: Cambridge University Press, 1985); Clifford Geertz, *The Interpretation of Cultures* (New York: Basic Books, 1973); Anthony Giddens, *New Rules of Sociological Method* (London: Hutchinson, 1976).

8. Peter Winch, *The Idea of a Social Science* (London: Routledge and Kegan Paul, 1958).

9. Noncommunicative research methods are not appropriate for moral development research, for example. Habermas's work happens to incorporate many of the precepts and research goals of Lawrence Kohlberg, a well known moral development researcher. See Kohlberg (1981).

10. See, for example, Herbert Marcuse, *One-Dimensional Man* (Boston: Beacon Press, 1964), pp. 157–158.

11. Lessnoff, "Technique, Critique and Social Science," p. 95.

12. See, for example, the contributions to *Social Science as Moral Inquiry,* ed. Norma Haan, et al. (New York: Columbia University Press, 1983); H. Garfinkel, *Forms of Explanation,* (New Haven: Yale University Press, 1981).

13. The 1981 Budget Revision document at NIMH, from directives of the Office of Management and Budget. As reported by Troy Duster in *Cultural Perspectives on Biological Knowledge,* ed. T. Duster and K. Garrett (Norwood, N.J.: Ablex Publishing Co., 1984), pp. 14–15.

14. To be fair, it must be admitted that the contemporary view of physical laws and theories has changed. Consider for example Nancy Cartwright, *How the Laws of Physics Lie* (Oxford: Oxford University Press, 1983).

15. *On the Logic of the Social Sciences,* 52–53.

16. Ibid., pp. 100–101.

17. This point is taken from Seyla Benhabib's synopsis of Habermas's early essays, in *Critique, Norm, and Utopia* (New York: Columbia University Press, 1986), p. 283.

18. Habermas, *Toward a Rational Society* (Boston: Beacon Press, 1970), pp. 62–80.

19. For example, G. A. Cohen, *Marx's Theory of History* (Oxford: Oxford University Press, 1978).

20. Jon Elster argues for the scientific status of the use of economic rationality in historical explanation in *Explaining Technical Change* (Cambridge: Cambridge University Press, 1983).

21. For an excellent and concise definition of the term *philosophy of the subject* in the Hegelian tradition see Seyla Benhabib, *Critique, Norm, and Utopia,* p. 54.

22. The German *aufheben* (literally, "to suspend") implies in Hegel's usage the synthesis (or reconciliation) of opposed principles. Such a synthesis is necessarily transformative; it is not merely a compromise.

23 See p. 40, *PDM.* Habermas refers here to Hegel's *Jenenser Realphilosophie,* ed. J. Hoffmeister (Leipzig: 1931), p. 248.

24. Friedrich Nietzsche, *On the Advantage and Disadvantage of History for Life* (Cambridge: 1980), p. 24.

25. Ibid.

26. Friedrich Nietzsche, *The Birth of Tragedy,* trans. Francis Golffing (Garden City, N.Y.: Doubleday and Co., 1956), p. 22.

27. Georges Bataille, *Der Heilige Eros* (Frankfurt am Main: 1982), p. 59. As cited in *PDM,* 231–232, interpolations are Habermas's.

28 This argument is developed in Foucault's *Surveiller et Punir;* in English: *Discipline and Punish: The Birth of the Prison,* trans. Alan Sheridan (New York: Random Press, 1979).

29. Habermas could develop his response further by examining the relationship of power, in Foucault's work, to knowledge. Although Foucault appears to speak as though power and knowledge are interdependent, his explanations of their relationship to each other is inadequate, given the deep issues raised by the concept of power-knowledge.

30. Thomas Flynn developed a response to this objection and the objections later that, in his view, gives a fairer account than Habermas's of Foucault's position, in "Foucault and the Politics of Postmodernity," *Nous* 23 (1989), pp. 187–198.

31. *PDM,* 284. Habermas notes that Nancy Fraser clarifies this inconsistency to some extent in her paper "Foucault's Body-Language: A Posthumanistic Political Rhetoric?" *Salmagundi* 61 (1983): 55–70.

32. Michel Foucault, "Preface," Gilles Deleuze and Felix Guattari, *Anti-Oedipus: Capitalism and Schizophrenia,* trans. R. Hurley, Mark Seem, and Helen Lane (Minneapolis: University of Minnesota Press, 1983), p. xiii.

33. It often has been pointed out, for example, that the theoretical underpinnings of the American constitution derive in part (through Benjamin Franklin) from the theory and practice of the Iroquoian Confederacy, which was arguably closer to the ideal speech situation than to representative government.

34. "The New Obscurity: The Crisis of the Welfare State and the Exhaustion of Utopian Energies," reprinted in *The New Conservatism,* (Cambridge, Mass.: MIT Press, 1990), pp. 48–70.

35. Martin Heidegger, "Einleitung zu *Was ist Metaphysik?*" in *Wegmarken* (Frankfurt am Main: 1978) pp. 361ff. As cited in *PDM,* 132.

36. Not all scholars of Heidegger agree that his philosophy undergoes a "turn" after reaching a "dead end" in *Being and Time.* See for example David Krell, "Nietzsche in Heidegger's *Kehre,*" *The Southwestern Journal of Philosophy* 13, no. 2 (1975): 197–204.

37. Jacques Derrida, *Of Grammatology,* trans. Gayatri Spivak (Baltimore: Johns Hopkins Press, 1974), p. 20. As cited in *PDM,* 177.

38. See p. 63, *Of Grammatology.* Derrida draws from Saussure's distinction between the signifier as "sound-image" and the signified as concept, but the term *sound-image* is potentially misleading, because Saussure understands it as a phenomenologically "structured appearing" of sound and not merely as a particular sound.

39. Ibid., pp. 62, 64.

40. Ibid., p. 70.

41. Jonathan Culler, *On Deconstruction* (Ithaca: Cornell University Press, 1982), p. 150. As quoted in *PDM,* 193.

42. Ludwig Wittgenstein, *Philosophical Investigations.* For a development of this consequence, see Saul Kripke, *Wittgenstein: On Rules and Private Language* (Cambridge, Mass.: Harvard University Press, 1982).

43. Theodor Adorno, and Max Horkheimer, *Dialectic of Enlightenment* (New York: Continuum, 1982), p. xvi.

44. Ibid., p. 110.

45. Ibid., p. 6.

46. Jean-François Lyotard, *The Postmodern Condition,* trans. Bennington and Massumi (Minneapolis: University of Minnesota Press, 1984), pp. 77, 79.

47. David Ingram points out that Habermas also once accepted a view of art that is quite at odds with the aesthetic of the beautiful in *Habermas and the Dialectic of Reason* (New Haven, Conn.: Yale University Press, 1987), p. 185.

48. Richard Rorty, *Consequences of Pragmatism* (Minneapolis: University of Minnesota Press, 1982), pp. xii–xiii.

49. K. Baynes, J. Bohman, and T. McCarthy, Eds., *After Philosophy: End or Transformation?* (Cambridge, Mass.: MIT Press, 1987).

50. "Philosophy as Placeholder and Interpreter," in *MCCA.*

7. Critical Applications of the Theory

1. For example, in R. E. Young, "Critical Theory and Learning," *Education Theory* 38 (Winter 1988): 47–59; and "Moral Development, Ego Autonomy and Questions of Practicality in the Critical Theory of Schooling," *Education Theory* 38 (Fall 1988): 391–404. See also Dieter Misgeld, "Education and Cultural Invasion"; Ray Kemp, "Planning, Public Hearings, and the Politics of Discourse"; John Forester, "Critical Theory and Planning Practice"; and Peter Grahame, "Criticalness, Pragmatics, and Everyday Life," all in *Critical Theory and Public Life,* ed. John Forester (Cambridge: MIT Press, 1985); Terry Winant, "Bloodline," *Hypatia—Women's International Forum* (Spring1984).

2. For example, Hans Joas in "The Unhappy Marriage of Hermeneutics and Functionalism," *Praxis International* 8 (April 1988): 34–51; Steven Vogel, "Habermas and Science," *Praxis International* 8 (October 1988): 329–349.

3. Daniel Hallin, "Critical Theory and the Mass Media," in *Critical Theory and Public Life,* ed. John Forester (Cambridge, Mass.: MIT Press, 1985).

4. Nancy Fraser, *Unruly Practices* (Minneapolis: University of Minnesota Press, 1989).

5. Philip Wexler, *Critical Social Psychology* (Boston: Routledge and Kegan Paul, 1983), see pp. 14–15.

6. Hallin, "Critical Theory and the Mass Media," p. 123.

7. Ibid., p. 125.

8. Ibid., p. 134.

9. Fraser, *Unruly Practices,* pp. 115-116.

10. Fraser adopts the term *the social* from Hannah Arendt, who noticed but disapproved of the rise of "needs talk" and its blurring effect on the "public-private" distinction. See ibid., Chapter 8, section 1.

11. Ibid., pp. 127–128.

12. See for example Wexler, *Critical Social Psychology,* Chapter 3.

13. Ibid., p. 30.

14. Ibid., pp. 29, 47, 51.

15. M. Horkeimer and T. Adorno, *The Dialectic of the Enlightenment* (New York: Continuum, 1982).

16. Ibid., p. 39

17. Ibid., pp. 46–47.

18. Ibid., p. 50.

19. Ibid., Part 3.

20. Ibid., pp. 69–70.

21. J. Habermas, "The New Obscurity," *Philosophical and Social Criticism* 2, no. 2 (Winter 1986); reprinted in *The New Conservatism: Culture, Criticism and the Historians' Debate,* ed. and trans. Shierry Weber Nicholson (Cambridge, Mass.: MIT Press, 1989).

22. Fraser, *Unruly Practices,* Chapter 8.

23. Habermas, "The New Obscurity," p. 15; insert mine.

24. Joel Whitebook, "Reconciling the Irreconcilable? Utopianism After Habermas," *Praxis International* 8, no. 1: 73–98.

Bibliography

Alexy, R. 1978. "Eine Theorie des Praktischen Diskurses." In W. Ölmüller, Ed., *Normenbegründung , normendurchsetzung.* Paderborn.

Apel, Karl-Otto. 1973. "Das Apriori der Kommunikationsgesellschaft." In Apel, Ed., *Transformation der Philosophie.* Frankfurt am Main: Suhrkamp Verlag.

———. 1976. "Das Problem der philosophischen Letztbegründung im Lichte einer transzendentalen Sprachpragmatik." In B. Kanitschneider, Ed. *Sprache und Erkenntnis.* Innsbruck.

Austin, J. L. 1962. *How to Do Things With Words,* ed. J. O. Urmson and Marina Sbisa, Cambridge, Mass.: Harvard University Press.

Bataille, Georges. 1982. *Der Heilige Eros.* Frankfurt am Main: Suhrkamp Verlag.

Baynes, Kenneth, James Bohman, and Thomas McCarthy, Eds. 1987. *After Philosophy: End or Transformation?* Cambridge, Mass.: MIT Press.

Bell, Daniel. 1976. *The Cultural Contradictions in Capitalism.* New York: Basic Books.

Benhabib, Seyla. 1986. *Critique, Norm, and Utopia.* New York: Columbia University Press.

Bernstein, Richard, Ed. 1985. *Habermas and Modernity.* Cambridge, Mass.: MIT Press.

Blumenberg, Hans. 1983. *The Legitimacy of the Modern Age,* general ed. Thomas McCarthy. Cambridge, Mass.: MIT Press.

Bohman, James. 1986. "Formal Pragmatics and Social Criticism." *Philosophy and Social Criticism* 11, no. 4: 331–353.

Chomsky, Noam. 1965. *Aspects of the Theory of Syntax.* Cambridge, Mass.: MIT Press.

Cohen, G. 1978. *Marx's Theory of History.* Oxford: Oxford University Press.

Culler, Jonathan. 1982. *On Deconstruction.* Ithaca: Cornell University Press.

Davidson, Donald. 1984. *Inquiries into Truth and Interpretation.* New York: Oxford University Press.

———. 1986. "A Coherence Theory of Truth and Knowledge." In *Truth and Interpretation: Perspectives on the Philosophy of Donald Davidson,* ed. Ernest Lepore. Oxford: Basil Blackwell.

Derrida, Jacques. 1974. *Of Grammatology.* Baltimore: Johns Hopkins University Press.

Dummett, Michael. 1975. "What Is a Theory of Meaning?" In Samuel Guttenplan, Ed., *Mind and Language.* Oxford: Clarendon Press.

Durkheim, Emile. 1965. *The Elementary Forms of Religious Life.* New York: Macmillan.

Elster, John. 1983. *Explaining Technical Change.* Cambridge: Cambridge University Press.

Flynn, Thomas. 1989. "Foucault and the Politics of Postmodernity." *Nous* 23: 187–98.

Forester, John, Ed. 1985. *Critical Theory and Public Life.* Cambridge, Mass.: MIT Press.

Foucault, Michel. 1979. *Discipline and Punish: The Birth of the Prison.* trans Alan Sheridan. New York: Random House.

———. 1983. "Preface." In Gilles Deleuze and Felix Guattari,

Anti-Oedipus: Capitalism and Schizophrenia, trans. R. Hurley, Mark Seem, and Helen Lane, trans. pp. xi–xiv. Minneapolis: University of Minnesota Press.

Fraser, Nancy. 1983. "Foucault's Body-Language: A Posthumanistic Political Rhetoric?" *Salmagundi* 61: 55–70.

———. 1987. "Women, Welfare and the Politics of Need Interpretation" in *Hypatia* 2, no. 1: 103–121.

———. 1989. *Unruly Practices.* Minneapolis: University of Minnesota Press.

Gadamer, Hans Georg. 1982. *Reason in the Age of Science,* general ed. Thomas McCarthy. Cambridge, Mass.: MIT Press.

Geertz, Clifford. 1973. *The Interpretation of Cultures.* New York: Basic Books.

Gehlen, Arnold. 1940. *Der Mensch.* Berlin. In English: *Man: His Nature and Place in the World.* New York: Columbia University Press, 1987.

Geuss, Raymond. 1981. *The Idea of a Critical Theory.* Cambridge: Cambridge University Press.

Giddens, Anthony. 1976. *New Rules of Sociological Method.* London: Hutchinson.

Grice, H. P. 1975. "Logic and conversation." In P. Cole, J. L. Morgan, Eds., *Syntax and Semantics 3: Speech Acts.* New York: Academic Press.

———. 1978. "Further Notes on Logic and Conversation." In P. Cole, Ed., *Syntax and Semantics 9: Pragmatics.* New York: Academic Press.

Grünbaum, Adolf. 1984. *The Foundations of Psychoanalysis: A Philosophical Critique.* Los Angeles: University of California Press.

Haack, Susan. 1978. "Theories of Truth." In *Philosophy of Logics.* Cambridge: Cambridge University Press.

Haan, Norma, Robert Bellah, Paul Rabinow, and William Sullivan, Eds. 1983. *Social Science as Moral Inquiry.* New York: Columbia University Press.

Habermas, Jürgen. 1970a. *Toward a Rational Society,* trans. Jeremy Shapiro. Boston: Beacon Press.

———. 1970b. "Towards a Theory of Communicative Competence." *Inquiry* 13, no. 4: 360–376.

———. 1973a. *Theory and Practice,* trans. John Viertel. Boston: Beacon Press.

———. 1973b. "A Postscript to *Knowledge and Human Interests.*" *Philosophy of the Social Sciences* 3, no. 2:157–89.

———. 1975. *Legitimation Crisis.* trans. Thomas McCarthy. Boston: Beacon Press. German: 1973.

———.1979. *Communication and the Evolution of Society.* trans. Thomas McCarthy. Boston: Beacon Press.

———. 1981. "Modernity Versus Postmodernity." *New German Critique* 22: 3–14.

———. 1983a. *Moralbewusstsein und kommunikatives Handeln.* Frankfurt am Main: Suhrkamp Verlag. In English: 1990.

———. 1983b. "Reply to Skjei." *Inquiry* 28: 105–22.

———. 1984a. *Vorstudien und Erganzungen zur Theorie des kommunikativen Handelns.* Frankfurt am Main: Suhrkamp Verlag.

———. 1984b. *The Theory of Communicative Action. Volume One: Reason and the Rationalization of Society,* trans. Thomas McCarthy. Boston: Beacon Press. German: 1981.

———. *Observations on "The Spiritual Situation of the Age,"* trans. Andrew Buchwalter. Cambridge, Mass.: MIT Press.

———. 1985a. *Die Neue Unübersichtlichkeit.* Frankfurt am Main: Suhrkamp Verlag.

———. 1985b. *Philosophical-political Profiles,* trans. Fred Lawrence. Cambridge, Mass.: MIT Press.

———. 1985c. "Questions and Counterquestions." In Richard Bernstein, Ed., *Habermas and Modernity.* Cambridge, Mass.: MIT Press.

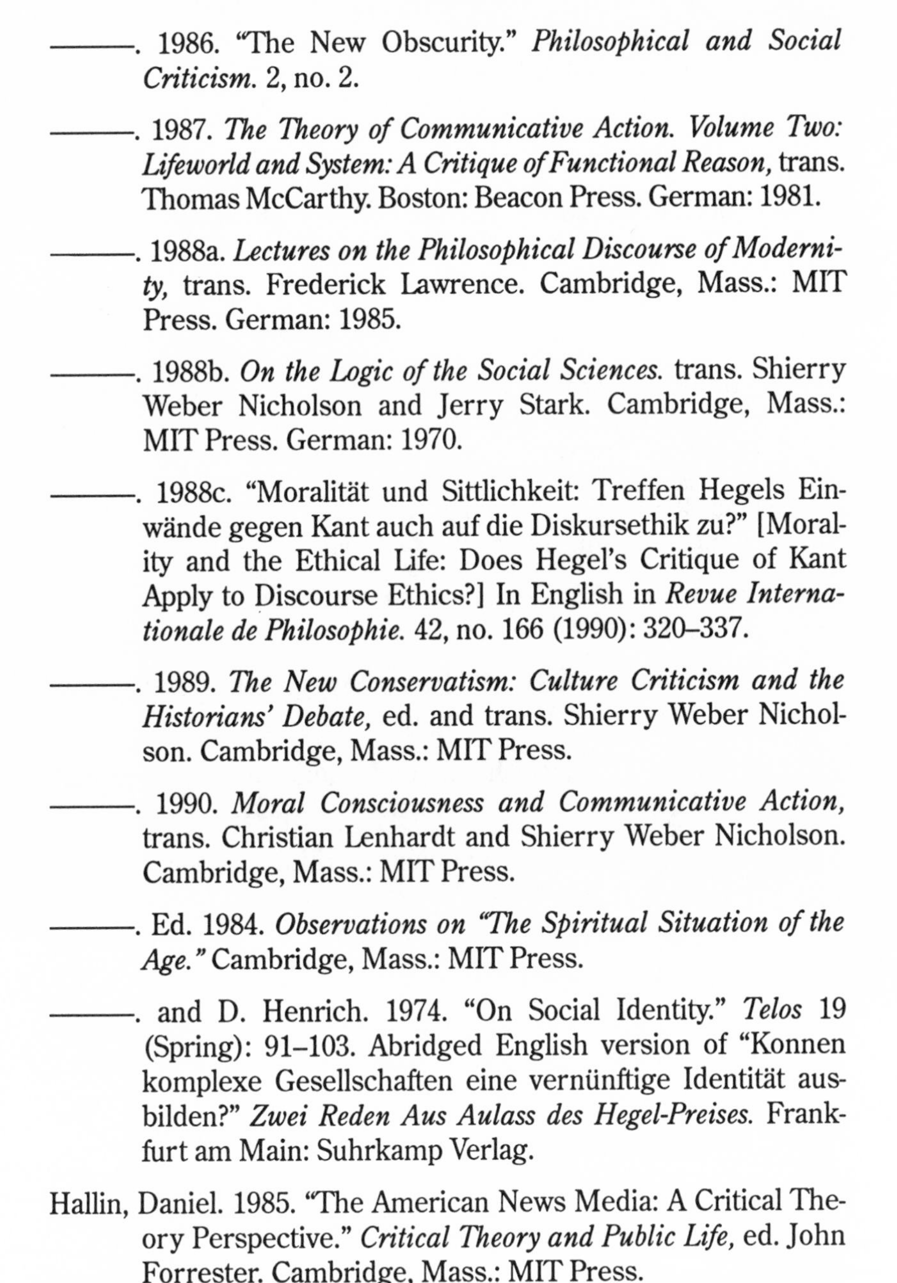

———. 1986. "The New Obscurity." *Philosophical and Social Criticism.* 2, no. 2.

———. 1987. *The Theory of Communicative Action. Volume Two: Lifeworld and System: A Critique of Functional Reason,* trans. Thomas McCarthy. Boston: Beacon Press. German: 1981.

———. 1988a. *Lectures on the Philosophical Discourse of Modernity,* trans. Frederick Lawrence. Cambridge, Mass.: MIT Press. German: 1985.

———. 1988b. *On the Logic of the Social Sciences.* trans. Shierry Weber Nicholson and Jerry Stark. Cambridge, Mass.: MIT Press. German: 1970.

———. 1988c. "Moralität und Sittlichkeit: Treffen Hegels Einwände gegen Kant auch auf die Diskursethik zu?" [Morality and the Ethical Life: Does Hegel's Critique of Kant Apply to Discourse Ethics?] In English in *Revue Internationale de Philosophie.* 42, no. 166 (1990): 320–337.

———. 1989. *The New Conservatism: Culture Criticism and the Historians' Debate,* ed. and trans. Shierry Weber Nicholson. Cambridge, Mass.: MIT Press.

———. 1990. *Moral Consciousness and Communicative Action,* trans. Christian Lenhardt and Shierry Weber Nicholson. Cambridge, Mass.: MIT Press.

———. Ed. 1984. *Observations on "The Spiritual Situation of the Age."* Cambridge, Mass.: MIT Press.

———. and D. Henrich. 1974. "On Social Identity." *Telos* 19 (Spring): 91–103. Abridged English version of "Konnen komplexe Gesellschaften eine vernünftige Identität ausbilden?" *Zwei Reden Aus Aulass des Hegel-Preises.* Frankfurt am Main: Suhrkamp Verlag.

Hallin, Daniel. 1985. "The American News Media: A Critical Theory Perspective." *Critical Theory and Public Life,* ed. John Forrester. Cambridge, Mass.: MIT Press.

Hare, R. M. 1952. *The Language of Morals.* Oxford: Clarendon Press.

Heidegger, Martin. 1962. *Being and Time.* trans. John Macquarrie and Edward Robinson. New York: Harper and Row.

Held, David. 1980. *Introduction to Critical Theory: Horkheimer to Habermas.* Berkeley: University of California Press.

Horkheimer, Max, and Theodor Adorno. 1982. *Dialectic of Enlightenment.* New York: Continuum.

Ingram, David. 1987. *Habermas and the Dialectic of Reason.* New Haven, Conn.: Yale University Press.

Jay, Martin. 1984. *Marxism and Totality: The Adventures of a Concept from Lukacs to Habermas.* Berkeley: University of California Press.

Joas, Hans. 1988. "The Unhappy Marriage of Hermeneutics and Functionalism." *Praxis International* 8: 34–51.

Kant, Immanuel. 1950. *Groundwork of the Metaphysics of Morals.* Chicago: University of Chicago Press.

Kohlberg, Lawrence. 1981. *The Philosophy of Moral Development.* San Fransisco: Harper and Row.

Krell, David. 1975. "Nietzsche in Heidegger's *Kehre.*" *Southwestern Journal of Philosophy* 13, no. 2:197–204.

Lessnoff, Michael. 1979. "Technique, Critique and Social Science." In *Philosophical Disputes in the Social Sciences,* ed. S. C. Brown. Atlantic Highlands, N.J.: Humanities Press.

Lyotard, Jean-François. 1984. *The Postmodern Condition,* trans. G. Bennington and B. Massumi. Minneapolis: University of Minnesota Press.

———. and Jean-Loup Thébaud. 1985. *Just Gaming,* trans. Wlad Godzich. Minneapolis: University of Minnesota Press.

Marcuse, Herbert. 1964. *One-Dimensional Man.* Boston: Beacon Press.

———. 1988. *Negations: Essays in Critical Theory,* with translations from the German by Jeremy Shapiro. London: Free Association Books.

Marx, Karl. 1973. *Grundrisse der Kritik der Politischen Ökonomie.* Harmondsworth, Middlesex: Penguin Books.

———. 1975. *Karl Marx: Early Writings,* ed. L. Colletti, trans. Rodney Livingstone and Gregor Benton. New York: McGraw Hill.

McCarthy, Thomas. 1978. *The Critical Theory of Jurgen Habermas.* Cambridge, Mass.: MIT Press.

McCarthy, Thomas, General editor. *Studies in Contemporary German Social Thought.* Cambridge, Mass.: MIT Press.

Mead, George Herbert. 1962. *Mind, Self and Society,* ed. C. Morris. Chicago: University of Chicago Press.

Nietzsche, Friedrich. 1956. *The Birth of Tragedy,* trans. Francis Golffing. Garden City, N.Y.: Doubleday and Co.

———. 1980. *On the Advantage and Disadvantage of History for Life,* ed. J. Keane. Indianapolis: Hackett Publishing Co.

Offe, Claus. 1984. *Contradictions of the Welfare State,* general ed. Thomas McCarthy. Cambridge, Mass.: MIT Press.

Papineau, David. 1978. *For Science in the Social Sciences.* New York: St. Martin's Press.

Parsons, Talcott. 1949. *The Structure of Social Action.* Glencoe, Ill.: Free Press.

———. 1977. *Social Systems and the Evolution of Action Theory.* New York: Free Press.

———. 1978. *Action Theory and Human Condition.* New York: Free Press.

Rawls, John. 1972. *A Theory of Justice.* Cambridge, Mass.: Harvard University Press.

Roderick, Rick. 1986. *Habermas and the Foundations of Critical Theory.* New York: St. Martin's Press.

Rorty, Richard. 1982. *Consequences of Pragmatism.* Minneapolis: University of Minnesota Press.

Ryle, Gilbert. 1946. "Knowing How and Knowing That." *Proceedings of the Aristotelian Society* 46.

Schutz, Alfred, and Thomas Luckmann. 1973. *The Structure of the Lifeworld.* Evanston, Ill.: Northwestern University Press.

Skjei, Erling. "A Comment on Performative, Subject, and Proposition in Habermas' Theory of Communication." *Inquiry* 28: 87–105.

Tar, Zoltan. 1985. *The Frankfurt School.* New York: Schocken Books.

Tarski, Alfred. 1935. "The Concept of Truth in Formalized Languages." Reprinted in A. Tarski. 1983. *Logic, Semantics, Metamathematics,* 2d ed., ed. John Corcoran. Indianapolis: Hackett Publishing Co.

Taylor, Charles. 1985. *Philosophical Papers, Volume Two: Philosophy and the Human Sciences.* Cambridge: Cambridge University Press.

Thompson, John B., and David Held, Eds. 1982. *Habermas: Critical Debates.* Cambridge, Mass.: MIT Press.

Toulmin, Stephen. 1964. *The Uses of Argument.* Cambridge: Cambridge University Press.

Vogel, Steven. 1988. "Habermas and Science." *Praxis International* 8: 329–349.

Weber, Max. 1904–1905. *Die protestantische Ethik und der Geist des Kapitalismus,* first published in the *Archiv für Sozialwissenschaft und Sozialpolitik,* 20–21. In English: *The Protestant Ethic and the Spirit of Capitalism.* New York: Charles Scribner's Sons, 1958.

Wellmer, Albrecht. 1986. *Ethik und Dialog.* Frankfurt am Main: Suhrkamp Verlag.

Wexler, Philip. 1983. *Critical Social Psychology.* Boston: Routledge and Kegan Paul.

White, Stephen. 1988. *The Recent Work of Jürgen Habermas.* New York: Cambridge University Press.

Whitebook, Joel. 1989. "Reconciling the Irreconcilable? Utopianism After Habermas." *Praxis International* 8, no. 1: 73–98.

Winant, Terry. 1984. "Bloodline." *Hypatia—Women's International Forum.*

Winch, Peter. 1958. *The Idea of a Social Science.* London: Routledge and Kegan Paul.

Young, R. E. 1988. "Critical Theory and Learning." *Education Theory* 38: 47–59.

———. 1988b. "Moral Development, Ego Autonomy and Questions of Practicality in the Critical Theory of Schooling." *Education Theory* 38 :391–404.

Index